The Late Henry Moss

Sam Shepard was born in 1943 in Fort Sheridan, Illinois. He moved to New York from California just as the off-Broadway theatre scene was emerging. He has written more than forty plays, of which eleven have won 'Obie' awards, besides collections of stories, prose writing and screenplays. His plays include *Buried Child, Simpatico, Curse of the Starving Class, True West, Fool for Love, A Lie of the Mind, States of Shock* and *The God of Hell.* His screenplay for *Paris, Texas* won the Golden Palm Award at the 1984 Cannes Film Festival and he directed his own screenplay, *Far North*, in 1988. A member of the American Academy of Arts and Letters, Shepard received the Gold Medal for Drama from the Academy in 1992, and in 1994 he was inducted into the Theatre Hall of Fame.

D1637605

also by Sam Shepard and available from Methuen

Sam Shepard Plays: 1
(The Unseen Hand, The Rock Garden, Chicago,
Icarus's Mother, 4-H Club, Fourteen Hundred Thousand,
Red Cross, Cowboys #2, Forensic & the Navigators,
The Holy Ghostly, Operation Sidewinder,
The Mad Dog Blues, Back Bog Beast Bait, Killer's Head)

Sam Shepard Plays: 3
(A Lie of the Mind, States of Shock, Simpatico)

A Lie of the Mind

The God of Hell

Sam Shepard

The Late Henry Moss

Methuen Drama

Published by Methuen 2006

1 3 5 7 9 10 8 6 4 2

First published in the United Kingdom in 2006 by
Methuen Publishing Limited
11–12 Buckingham Gate
London SW1E 6LB

Methuen Publishing Limited Reg. No. 3543167

A CIP catalogue record for this book is available from
the British Library

ISBN 0 413 77589 5
978 0413 77589 4

Typeset by Country Setting, Kingsdown, Kent
Printed and bound in Great Britain by
Cox and Wyman Ltd, Reading, Berkshire

The Late Henry Moss

The Late Henry Moss was first produced by the Magic Theatre, San Francisco, on 7 November 2000. The cast was as follows:

Ray Moss	Sean Penn
Earl Moss	Nick Nolte
Henry Moss	James Gammon
Conchalla	Sheila Tousey
Esteban	Cheech Marin
Taxi Driver	Woody Harrelson
Funeral Attendant 1	Rod Gnapp
Funeral Attendant 2	Dennis Ludlow

Director	Sam Shepard
Designer	Andy Stacklin
Costumes	Christine Dougherty
Lighting	Anne Militello
Composer and music archivist	T Bone Burnett
Choreography	Peter Pucci
Stage management	Michael Svenkel

The Late Henry Moss had its European premiere at the Almeida Theatre, London, on 12 January 2006. The cast was as follows:

Ray Moss	Andrew Lincoln
Earl Moss	Brendan Coyle
Henry Moss	Trevor Cooper
Conchalla	Flaminia Cinque
Esteban	Simon Gregor
Taxi Driver	Jason Watkins
Funeral Attendant 1	Martin Barron
Funeral Attendant 2	Curtis Jordan

Director	Michael Attenborough
Designer	Robert Jones
Lighting	Mark Henderson
Composer & Sound Designer	Adam Cork
Choreographer	Lynne Page
Casting	Lisa Makin
Fight Coordinator	Terry King
Dialect Coach	Penny Dyer

Prelude to Act One (Drunken Rhumba)

Lights go to black on set. In the dark, very sultry Mexican rhumba music comes up. A white spotlight hits the couple of **Henry Moss** *and* **Conchalla** *wrapped in a tight embrace, cheek to cheek. They are amazingly drunk and yet synchronized in tight, fluid coordination with only the occasional stumble and foot crunch to give them away. They begin extreme down left on the apron in front of the set and career their way across the stage, doing a couple of twirls and deep waist-bends along the way. Their cheeks stay pressed together the whole time, and they seem oblivious to the world. The dance is brief and somewhat shocking. They disappear off right. Spotlight goes to black, then lights ease up on set to begin Act One.*

Act One

Scene: Night. A run-down adobe dwelling on the outskirts of Bernalillo, New Mexico. The roof is open; just bare, rough-plastered walls. A mesquite door with black iron hinges in stage right wall. A deep-silled window up right. A single cotlike bed set horizontally into a small alcove, center of upstage wall with a small barred window directly above it, like a jail cell. There is a blue curtain on a rod in front of the bed that can be opened or closed by hand and sometimes mechanically. The curtain is open for now, revealing the corpse of **Henry Moss**, *a man in his late sixties. He lies face up on the bed with the crown of his head toward stage right. A heavy Mexican blanket in yellow and red designs covers him from the forehead down to his ankles. Over the blanket a white sheet has been spread smoothly. Only the top of* **Henry**'s *head and his bare feet are revealed. Nothing is seen of his face. There is an old-style bathtub with claw feet upstage left of the bed. A sink, gas stove and small refrigerator are set against upstage wall; all very run-down and dirty. Extreme downstage left of center is a simple round Formica table with two metal S-shaped chairs set across from each other; one upstage right, the other downstage left.* **Earl Moss**, **Henry**'s *elder son, sits in the downstage chair with his back partially to audience, thumbing through an old photo album of* **Henry**'s, *studying the pictures.* **Ray Moss**, **Earl**'s *younger brother, stands upstage of the table, facing the audience and idly going through an old red tool chest of* **Henry**'s *placed on the table in front of*

him. A bottle of bourbon sits in the center of table with two plastic cups.
An ashtray; cigarettes. Nothing else. Long pause after lights come up as
Earl *thumbs through album,* **Ray** *fiddles with tools.*

Earl (*thumbing through album*)   Well, you know me, Ray – I was
never one to live in the past. That was never my deal. You
know – you remember how I was.

Ray   Yeah. Yeah, right. I remember.

Earl   But, these days now – I don't know. Something like this –
outta the blue. Maybe it's age or something.

Ray   Age?

Earl   Yeah.

Ray   Whose age?

Earl   Mine.

Ray   Oh. I thought you meant his.

Earl   No – me. Gettin' older. You know. I mean at eighteen,
nineteen, my mind was going in a whole different direction.
You remember how I was. (*He suddenly sings.*)

Gonna tie my pecker to a tree, to a tree.
Gonna tie my pecker to a tree.

You remember that? (*Pause.* **Ray** *just stares at him.*) Well, do ya?

Ray   I thought that was him. I remember him singing that.

Earl   That was me!

Ray   Oh.

Earl   1956, '57? When was that?

Ray   What?

Earl   When I used to come home singing that.

Ray   I don't know. Musta been later.

Earl   Not that much later. Couldn't a been. Ripple wine and
Mexican Benzedrine! Those were high times, Ray! High old
times.

Pause.

Ray   I remember you leaving. That's all I remember.

Earl (*looking up at* **Ray**)   What? When?

Ray   When you first left. When the big blowout happened.

Earl   Big blowout?

Ray   You know what I'm talkin' about.

Pause. **Earl** *stares at him.*

Earl   Ooh – that. Way back.

Ray   Yeah.

Earl   Way, way back.

Ray   That's still very vivid with me. Like it happened yesterday.

Earl (*going back to album*)   You shouldn't let that stuff haunt you, Ray.

Ray   I remember the windows exploding.

Earl   Exploding?

Ray   Blown out. Glass everywhere.

Earl   Ooh – yeah. That was *him* – (*Gestures to* **Henry**.) not me. That was him doing that.

Ray   Yeah. Him.

Earl   You're getting me mixed up with him.

Ray   No I'm not. I know it was him.

Earl   Well, don't get me mixed up with him.

Ray   I'm not. I know it was him.

Earl   Good.

Pause. He thumbs through album.

He was the one breaking windows. Not me.

Ray   I know that. (*Pause.*) What brought it on exactly? That was never very clear to me.

Earl   Oh, come on, Ray –

Ray   What?

Earl   You mean after all this time – after all these years – you still don't know?

Ray   No. I never knew.

Earl   She locked him out of the house. You knew that, didn't you?

Ray   Um – I don't know. Yeah, I guess.

Earl   Set him right off. Went into one of his famous Wild Turkey storms. You knew all about that.

Ray   I remember it like a war or something. An invasion.

Earl   Yeah, well, things get embellished over the years. You were a kid.

Ray   So were you.

Earl   Yeah, but there was a certain – maturity about me. I was coming into my own back then.

Ray   Explosions. Screaming. Smoke. The telephone.

Earl   Explosions? There weren't any explosions, Ray.

Ray   People running. You were one of them.

Earl   What?

Ray   Running.

Earl   I never ran!

Ray   Mom was running.

Earl   He had her trapped in the kitchen! Under the sink! How could she run? Huh? How could she possibly run? You've really got this screwed up, Ray. You oughta get this straightened out, you know. It's time you got it straight. It's no good carrying the wrong pictures around with you the rest of your life. They're liable to get more and more warped as time goes on. Pretty soon you'll start to forget how it really was.

Ray   You ran. I watched you.

Earl   I never ever ran!

Ray   You climbed into that '51 Chevy and took off. That was the last I saw of you for seven years. Things like that you don't forget. They mark time. For *me* they do.

Earl (*returns to album*)   Yeah, well – I never ran, I'm not a runner. Never have been. (*Pause.*)

Ray   Seven years. Thought I'd never see you again. I thought about you all the time but I bet I never once crossed your mind. Never once.

Earl   That's not true.

Ray   Maybe once.

Earl   Once or twice.

Ray   Once, maybe.

Earl   I sent you something every Christmas. Most every Christmas, I did.

Ray   Yeah.

Earl   Socks. T-shirts. Rubbers. I sent you Camels once.

Ray   Tokens. Tokens of guilt.

Earl (*looking up*)   Guilt? Look – buddy boy, I had a lot on my mind back then.

Ray   Yeah.

Earl   I was heading somewhere.

Long pause. **Earl** *goes back to album.* **Ray** *fiddles with tools.*

Ray   What should we do with his tools?

Earl   You want 'em? You might as well keep 'em.

Ray I don't work with my hands anymore.

Earl Oh? Since when?

Ray I don't know. It just faded.

Earl That's a shame, Ray. You were good with your hands. You used to be under a car all day long.

Ray What car?

Earl Some car. I don't know what car. Some car or other.

Ray I never had a car.

Earl Well, whose car was it, then, you were always working under?

Ray It was his car.

Earl Okay.

Ray It wasn't my car.

Earl Fine.

Ray Well, it wasn't. I never had a car. You were the one with the car.

Earl All right! It was *his* car, it wasn't your car! Who gives a flying fuck whose car it was! I just seem to remember, Ray, that you always liked working on cars and I thought you might like to have the tools in case you wanted to pursue that. That's all. Simple as that.

Long pause. **Earl** *goes back to album.* **Ray** *handles tools.*

Ray Looks like they're all pretty cheap anyway. Taiwan steel. Swap-meet stuff.

Earl You oughta keep 'em, Ray. For his sake you oughta keep 'em.

Ray For his sake?

Earl Yeah.

Ray He's dead.

Earl   I know he's dead.

Ray   So why should he care?

Earl   He won't care, Ray.

Ray   So it'd be for *my* sake, not his sake.

Earl   Yeah. For your sake. You never can tell when the urge might come up again.

Ray   What urge?

Earl   To work with your hands! That urge! The urge to be useful again.

Pause.

Ray (*looking at tools*)   They're not worth diddly.

Earl   That's not really the point, is it, Ray? I mean, nothing he's got is worth diddly. Not like we're inheriting a legacy here.

Ray   Ratchet's pretty nice.

He picks up a very large ratchet wrench and fits a socket onto it.

Earl   Why don't you keep that, then? He'd like that, Ray.

Ray   Keep the ratchet?

Earl   Yeah. Keep the ratchet. It's a nice one, right?

Ray   A single big-ass ratchet? What am I gonna do with a single ratchet?

Earl   Work on your Buick! I don't know.

Ray   I don't have a Buick.

Earl   Goddammit, Ray!

Ray   Well, I don't. You want me to say I have a Buick just so you can feel good about giving me these crummy tools? They're not your tools anyway. You don't own the tools.

Earl   I know I don't own the tools!

Ray   They're his tools.

Earl   I know that.

Ray   They're not yours to give away.

Earl   They're not yours either!

Ray   They're nobody's tools!

Ray *slams the wrench back into the toolbox. Long pause.* **Earl** *goes back to album.* **Ray** *turns upstage and stares at* **Henry**'*s corpse, then turns back to* **Earl**.

Ray   Well, don't you think it's about time we notified someone? We can't just sit around here. Who're you supposed to call first? The cops?

Earl   The cops? What're you thinking about?

Ray   Who, then? The mortician? The Chamber of Commerce? Who?

Earl (*back on album*)   I'm not ready yet. (*Pause.*)

Ray   *You're* not ready?

Earl   No. I'm not.

Ray   Well, how long are we gonna wait?

Earl (*looks up*)   What's the rush? Huh? I'd like to spend a little time with him if you don't mind.

Ray   Time?

Earl   Yeah, time. Before he's rushed off and processed into the funeral business. Before they apply the makeup and formaldehyde and dress him up in his Air Force khakis.

Ray   Well, how much time do you need, Earl?

Earl   I'll let you know.

Ray   Haven't you been sitting here with him for a long time already?

Earl   I'll let you know, Ray.

Ray   What've you been doing just sitting here with him all this time?

Earl   Nothing.

Ray   Have you been talking to him, Earl?

Earl   He's dead.

Ray   Yeah, but when you're alone like this – just sitting here – just the two of you – you can start to make stuff up.

Earl   What stuff?

Ray   Stuff in your head. You can start – imagining things.

Earl   Like what?

Ray   Well, like for instance – you could imagine that he's still alive; he can still hear you – Maybe it's even better that way.

Earl   What way?

Ray   Imagining. I mean that might be even better than if he were actually alive because now you can really tell him things. You can tell him all kinds of things that you couldn't tell him before because now he's dead and you're imagining him to be alive and there's nothing he can do about it but listen.

Earl   I wasn't talking to him, all right! I wasn't imagining anything! I was just sitting here! Alone. With him. Just sitting here in the dark. Alone.

Pause. **Ray** *turns upstage and starts to move slowly toward* **Henry**'s *body.*

Ray   We can't just bury him ourselves, huh? Just dig a hole and do it ourselves? That's illegal, isn't it?

Earl   Yeah, every death has to be reported these days. Unless you kill somebody.

Ray   We could report it *after* we bury him.

Earl   They'd just dig him back up.

Ray   I mean, that's what you'd do with a dog –

Earl   What?

Ray   Just dig a hole and bury him.

Earl Yeah.

Ray So how come you can't do that with a father?

He moves in closer to **Henry***'s corpse.* **Earl** *pours himself a drink, smokes and keeps thumbing through album.*

Earl I don't know. I don't know the answer to that, Ray. I don't know why that is. Nobody cares about a dog. I guess that's it.

Ray (*getting very close to* **Henry**)   Nobody cares about a dog.

Earl Well, they don't.

Ray You mean outside the dog's little circle of friends? His little family.

Earl Yeah, nobody cares.

Ray *reaches out to touch* **Henry***'s corpse.* **Earl** *stands suddenly.*

Earl Don't touch him!

Long pause. **Ray** *stares at* **Earl**.

Ray What?

Earl Just don't touch him.

Ray Why is that, Earl?

Earl Just – don't. It's not a good idea.

Pause. **Ray** *looks at the corpse, then back at* **Earl**.

Ray Am I gonna catch something – some disease?

Earl Just – get away from him.

Ray Have *you* touched him?

Earl No.

Ray It's not gonna hurt anything, is it?

He goes to touch the corpse again, but **Earl** *makes a strong move toward him.*

Earl Don't touch him, Ray!

Ray *backs off.*

Ray   What're you so jumpy about?

Earl   I'm not jumpy.

Ray   Are you superstitious or something?

Earl   I just don't think it's a good idea to touch him.

Ray   Afraid he might come back to life?

Earl   That's pretty funny.

Pause.

Ray   He's starting to stink, Earl. I think he's starting to stink.

Earl   I can't smell it.

Ray   Yeah, well, you've been with him too long. You've grown insensitive to it.

Earl   Insensitive. *Me,* insensitive?

Ray   Yeah. There's a stink in here. There's definitely a stink and you can't smell it.

Earl   That's right.

Ray   How long's it take before things really start to rot? You know –

Earl   How should I know? I'm no expert on death.

He returns to table, sits and goes back to album.

Ray   I mean really bad – turning to maggots.

Earl   We're not gonna wait *that* long, for Christ's sake! Just try to relax a little, Ray. All right? Just relax. Feel honored that we have this small time alone with him. Try to treasure it.

Pause.

Ray   Honored?

Earl   That's right, *honored.* Somebody else could've discovered him first. Anybody. A total stranger. The taxi driver or that crazy chick – what's her name – or – anybody. They'd have called the cops right off the bat. The mortuary boys would've been here already with a body bag and hauled him off. And there we'd be. We'd be the last ones notified. No privacy. All kinds of questions. Forms to fill out. We'd never have had two seconds with him by ourselves.

Pause.

Ray   What taxi driver?

Earl   What?

Ray   What taxicab driver?

Earl   The taxicab driver. The guy who picked him up and took him fishing. The guy who brought him back.

Ray   Same guy?

Earl   Yeah. Same guy. I told you that. I told you all about that on the phone.

Ray   Well, if he picked him up and brought him back, how would he have discovered him dead? He would've had to die in the taxi.

Earl   I was just saying that as an example!

Ray   It's not a good one.

Earl   I was just using the taxicab driver as an example of anyone! How it could've been anyone other than us who found him first!

Ray   Who did find him first?

Earl   *I* found him first! I told you that. You never listen.

Ray   And you just decided to sit here with him.

Earl   Sit here until you got here. I figured it was my duty.

Ray   Your duty?

Earl   That's right, my duty.

Ray   'Duty and honor, duty and honor.' Doo-wah, doo-wah, doo-wah duty.

Earl   Go fuck yourself, Ray. (*Pause.* **Earl** *goes through album.*)

Ray   So, who's this crazy chick?

Earl   What?

Ray   This crazy chick you mentioned as one of the possible candidates who might've found him first?

Earl   His girlfriend.

Ray   His girlfriend?

Earl   Yeah. Whatever her name was – 'Conchita' or something.

Ray   'Conchita'?

Earl   Something like that.

Ray   'Conchita Banana'?

Earl   Don't get cute. Have some respect for the dead. I went through all this stuff with you before on the phone. Don't you ever listen to anything?

Ray   I was in shock.

Earl   Well, snap out of it!

Pause. **Ray** *slowly circles table around* **Earl**'s *back, then returns to the chair across from* **Earl** *and slowly sits. He pours himself a drink.*

Ray (*as he crosses behind* **Earl**)   I'm still in shock. I wasn't expecting to be in shock but I guess that's the thing about shock.

Earl   What?

Ray   It's unexpected, you don't see it coming. You just find yourself in the grips of it. You do the best you can.

Earl (*focused on album*)   Why don't we take a walk or something, Ray? This New Mexican air might just do us some good.

Ray (*seated with drink*)   I know this is probably going to irritate you a whole lot, Earl, but would you mind going back through the whole story for me one more time?

Earl   What story?

Ray   The stuff this guy – what's his name? The neighbor?

Earl   Esteban?

Ray   Yeah – Esteban. That's it. The stuff this guy, Esteban, told you on the phone when he called you in New York. *Before* you found Dad dead. What happened just before? I'm a little lost here.

Pause. **Earl** *pushes the album away and with a long exhale, stares at his brother.*

Earl   What's the matter with you?

Ray   Me? Nothing. Nothing's the matter with me. I'm his son. You're his son. I've got a right to know, as much as you do. We're both blood.

Earl   I told you everything already, once!

Ray   Yeah – yeah, you did. But there's some stuff that doesn't make sense.

Earl   What stuff!

Ray   There's all these – all these people you mentioned. It's just too – stupid! It's stupid that he died like this! Out here in the middle of nowhere with no – contact. No contact whatsoever!

Earl   That's the way he *lived*! He lived with no contact. Why shouldn't he die the same way?

Pause. **Ray** *drops his head slowly and stares at the table.* **Earl** *stares at him.*

Earl   All right – all right. Once more and that's it. I can't keep going through this, Ray. It's not something I enjoy.

Ray   Why would you enjoy it?

Earl   I *don't* enjoy it! That's what I'm saying.

Ray   Then why even bring it up?

Earl   Goddammit, Ray, you are such a little piss-ant.

Ray   That may be. That may well be. A 'piss-ant'. I'd just like to hear the story again, Earl. The whole story.

Pause. **Earl** *stares at him, then begins.*

Earl   I got the phone call. Collect. Esteban says he's worried about the old man.

Ray   This was a week ago or something?

Earl   That's right. A week ago. About a week. Before I called you. Now listen up! Try to pay attention this time.

Ray   I'm all ears.

Earl   He's worried – Esteban. He's the neighbor. He says Dad got some money in the mail. Henry's cashed a check that came in and he's walking around with this cash burning a hole in his pocket.

Ray   Where'd the check come from?

Earl   Who knows. GI check or something. Government pension. I guess he was always getting these checks and going on binges. He's buying booze with it. He gets a haircut. He hitchhikes down to the shopping center. He wanders around downtown, drunk. Then he wanders down to the gas station and buys a fishing license.

Ray   Drunk?

Earl   Yeah, drunk. What else? Then he hitchhikes back out here and calls a taxi from Albuquerque. Taxi picks him up and he takes off for a day and goes fishing. He comes back that night with this Indian chick.

Ray   The crazy one?

Earl   The crazy one.

Ray *motions for* **Earl** *to continue.*

Earl   So, the taxi waits for him and the woman. Esteban sees the cab outside, so he comes over with some soup.

Ray Soup?

Earl That's right. Soup, Ray. That's exactly right. Esteban was always bringing Henry soup or chili or some damn thing. Trying to sober him up. Esteban says the woman's in the bathtub, giggling. She's half-naked and drunker than skunk. Esteban drinks with them but Dad won't eat the soup. They have a big argument about the soup and Henry kicks him out. Esteban stays outside by his trailer and keeps watching the house. He sees Henry come out with the Indian woman wrapped in a blanket. She's still giggling. They pile into the taxi and take off. That was the last he saw of him.

Ray So when you get here, after the phone call from this neighbor – I mean, I'm trying to put this all together – how many days did it take you to get here?

Earl You mean after the phone call?

Ray Yeah.

Earl I don't know – three or four.

Ray Three or four days?

Earl Yeah. I guess. I don't know.

Ray It took you three or four days after you hear that he's in trouble?

Earl I had some business to take care of!

Ray Business? What kinda business, Earl?

Earl Packaging! I got a packaging business now. We make boxes.

Ray So after your 'packaging business' you fly down here, walk in the door and find Henry dead in his bed? Is that it?

Earl Yeah. That's it! Just like that. Just how he is right there. I haven't touched him. He was laying there stroked out on his back just like he is right now. All I did was cover him up.

Long awkward pause. **Ray** *gets up and goes to the window. He stares out.* **Earl** *watches him.*

Earl   So – how's the family?

Ray *doesn't move from window. Keeps his back to* **Earl***.*

Ray   What family?

Earl   Your family. Out west.

Ray   I don't have a family.

Earl   Oh – I thought you got married and, uh – somewhere I heard you got married.

Ray   I never had a family.

Earl   Oh –

Ray *turns toward* **Earl** *but stays near window.*

Ray   How's *your* family?

Earl   I don't have one either. You know that.

Ray   How am I supposed to know that?

Earl   Have I ever mentioned a family to you?

Ray   No – but I thought maybe –

Earl   Maybe what?

Ray   Maybe you had a secret family.

Earl   A secret family?

Ray   Yeah.

Pause.

No?

Earl   No.

Ray   That's too bad, Earl.

Earl   If I had a secret family, why would I tell you about it?

Ray   Because I'm your buddy, Earl. I'm your little buddy. You can tell me all your secrets.

Pause.

Earl   Look, Ray – there wasn't much either one of us could do about this. You know that. He was on his way out. Been that way for a long time. Pickled. Pissing blood. The shakes. Blackouts. Hallucinations. There was all kind of signs.

Ray   Signs.

Earl   Yeah. He stopped eating for one thing.

Pause. **Ray** *crosses over to refrigerator and opens it. It's completely empty except for a small jar of jalapeño peppers.* **Ray** *takes the jar out, closes fridge, crosses to table and sets jar on it*

Ray   Jalapeños.

Earl   Can't stay alive on peppers and hooch.

Ray *opens jar, sits at table and starts eating the peppers, chasing them down with bourbon.*

Ray   How do we get ahold of this taxicab driver?

Earl   What?

Ray   The taxicab driver who took Dad fishing.

Earl   You got me. You have to find out what company it was first.

Ray   Well, Esteban would know that, wouldn't he? The friendly neighbor? He saw the cab.

Earl   Well, yeah, but – good luck finding the driver.

Ray   Shouldn't be that hard. They keep records. Every car has a number. Every driver. It's the law. They log in, they log out.

Earl   What's the taxicab driver gonna tell you?

Ray   I dunno. Something. Maybe he saw something.

Earl *slides the album toward him, showing him an old photo of their father as a boy.* **Ray** *doesn't look at it: just keeps chewing on jalapeños.*

Earl   Look at this. Here he is with his dog, Gyp. Look at that. '1931', it says. 1931. So, he's how old there? How old would he have been?

Ray   Maybe he'd know how to find that Indian woman.

Earl (*still with album photo*)   Well, let's see — that's thirty — no — fifty-seven years ago? So — fifty-seven — he would've been — he would've been twelve years old there. Twelve years old! Imagine that!

Ray   Maybe she saw something.

Earl   So who's president then? Hoover? Or was it FDR?

Ray   Maybe she can tell us what happened.

Earl   Look at that. There he is. No idea what's in store for him. Just a kid standing in a wheat field with his dog.

Ray *slams the jar of jalapeños on the table and stands.*

Ray   Why did he suddenly take it into his head to go fishing, Earl? Why is that? You don't take a taxicab to go fishing! Why is he suddenly up in the mountains with an Indian chick fishing! It doesn't make any sense! I woulda gone fishing with him! Why didn't he call *me* to go fishing! I love to fish! Why didn't he call *me*?

Pause. **Earl** *just stares at him.*

Earl   You were far away, Ray.

Pause. Silence. The door swings open wide and **Esteban***, a small, skinny Mexican man in his fifties, very neatly dressed in khaki pants, light pink shirt with dark blue tie and shiny black shoes, is standing in the doorway holding a large green bowl of steaming soup with both hands. He smiles broadly at the brothers and just stays there in open doorway.* **Earl** *stands quickly from table and moves toward him.*

Earl   Esteban! Come on in.

Esteban   Is Mr Henry here? I saw the light on.

Earl   Come in, Esteban. Good to see you.

Esteban *begins to cross, very slowly, toward table, keeping his eyes glued to bowl of soup, careful not to spill a drop. It takes him a very long time to reach his destination.*

Esteban (*as he crosses slowly*)   I brought Mr Henry his soup. He sometimes will eat. Sometimes not. Depends on his mood. How you catch him. I was very worried this time. He just disappear like that.

Earl (*closing door*)   Esteban, this is my brother, Ray. He just – came in from California.

Esteban (*keeps moving, eyes fixed on bowl*)   Glad to meet you, Mr Ray. *Mucho gusto.*

Ray *nods, stays where he is by window.* **Earl** *crosses to table, ahead of* **Esteban***, and moves the album to make room for the soup's arrival.* **Esteban** *keeps smiling and inching slowly across the room with soup.*

Esteban (*crossing slowly*)   I put vegetables and chorizo in there for his blood. Habañeros. I know how the blood can get from liquor. I was a drinking man, myself. Many years. Oh, yes. They couldn't stop me. Nobody. Many people weep for me but I could not hear them. Bells rang in all the chapels but I was deaf.

Earl   Do you want me to take that for you, Esteban?

Esteban   No, no, no – I can manage, Mr Earl. Many bowls I have balanced across the road for Henry. Many years of practice. The timing I know by now. The soup it cools down just right from my trailer to his door. Henry no like it too hot. One time he burn himself so bad he almost kill me. It was funny but he almost did. I could see the murder in his eye. Real murder. The pain had made him crazy. I tell him, is such little pain, Mr Henry. Don't kill me for such a little pain as this. Wait for a bigger pain to kill me! (*He laughs, then stops himself when he sees he might spill the soup.*) But he was drunk – so he no laugh. He no laugh with me.

Ray   Who is this?

Earl   Ésteban. (*Pronounced incorrectly with accent on first syllable.*) The neighbor.

Esteban (*pronounced correctly*)   Estéban.

Earl (*repeats the mispronunciation*)   Ésteban.

Esteban *finally reaches the table and sets the soup down very carefully. He smiles and sighs with relief, then pulls a soup spoon and napkin out of his back pocket and sets them neatly beside the bowl. He pulls a salt-shaker out of his back pocket and places it in front of the soup. Pause.* **Earl** *looks at* **Ray**, *then back to* **Esteban**, *who is smiling broadly.*

Esteban   So – is Mr Henry home now from fishing? I was very glad to see the light here. Very, very happy. I was afraid he might just – vanish.

Earl   He's – he's sleeping, Esteban. Worn out, I guess.

Esteban (*looks toward* **Henry**'s *corpse*)   Ooh. (*Lowers his voice to a whisper.*) That is good. He need that. He need that after fishing.

Esteban *tiptoes over to* **Henry**'s *bed and looks at corpse.*

Earl   Don't, uh – don't disturb him now, Esteban.

Esteban (*keeping distance from* **Henry**)   Oh, no.

Ray   Yeah. Don't touch him, whatever you do. My brother's liable to go ape-shit.

He crosses to table, sits; pours a drink.

Esteban (*whispering, looking at* **Henry**)   No, he need sleep. He need plenty of that. More than soup, he need sleep.

Earl   Yeah, he could use some sleep.

Esteban   I bet you – (*He giggles.*) I bet you that big crazy woman wore him out. You know, Mr Earl? That Indian woman. (*Laughs.*) She is so – you know – (*Cups his hands under his chest.*) robusto! No? Very strong woman. Right, Mr Earl? A lot of woman for Henry.

Earl   Yeah – I don't know.

Esteban   He have fun with her I bet. (*Giggles and sways.*) She bend his back like a willow tree. She fuck him silly. (**Esteban** *bursts out laughing and jumping up and down.*)

Earl   Don't do that – Don't wake him up. Okay, Esteban?

Esteban *quiets down and goes back to whispering.* **Ray** *watches from the table, somewhat perplexed.*

Esteban   Oh, no. No, no, no. He need his sleep. That is good for Henry. I was so worried when I saw he have that money. So much money. That is why I call you, Mr Earl.

Earl   I'm glad you did, Esteban.

Esteban   So much money in his hand. It is no good when a man is fighting his weakness. Too much money.

He sneaks up closer to the bed and stares at the corpse.

He sleep very peaceful. Very still.

Earl   Yeah – He's exhausted.

Esteban   I can barely hear him breathe. Maybe the blanket's covering his nose too much.

Esteban *moves as though to lift the blanket away from* **Henry***'s face.* **Earl** *leaps at him.*

Earl   Don't touch him!

Esteban *leaps back away from* **Henry** *and stands there in shock. Pause.*

Ray (*to* **Esteban**)   I tried to warn you about that.

Earl   I'm sorry, Esteban – I'm just, uh – I'm a little worn out myself.

Esteban *stays frozen where he is, staring at* **Earl***.* **Earl** *moves toward* **Esteban** *but* **Esteban** *backs up from him.*

Earl   Why don't you, uh – have a seat or something. It's okay, Esteban. Everything's fine.

Pause. **Esteban** *keeps staring at* **Earl***.*

Ray   Esteban – you live right across the road here, is that right? You're the neighbor?

Esteban (*turning toward* **Ray**)   Yes, sir.

Ray   How long have you lived over there, Esteban?

Esteban   Thirty years.

Ray   Thirty years.

Esteban   *Más o menos.*

Ray   Thirty years in a trailer.

Esteban   Yes, sir, Mr Ray.

Ray   So, you've known my father for a good long time, then.

Esteban   Yes. Sir. Ever since he move here from California. When he have that bad time.

Ray   Which bad time was that, Esteban?

Esteban   When he think the world was trying to eat him.

Ray   What?

Esteban   When he think – he was doomed, he said.

Ray   He said that?

Esteban   Yes, sir. I have times like that myself but Henry never believe me. He think he was the only one.

Ray   Doomed?

Esteban   Yes, sir.

Ray   Can it with the 'sir' shit, all right! I'm not your 'sir'.

Earl   Take it easy, Ray.

Ray   Well, what does he think this is, the military or something? I don't need that 'sir' stuff.

Earl   He's just being polite, you idiot! It's a rare thing these days.

Ray   Polite?

Earl   Politeness. It's okay, Esteban. (*Pause.*)

Ray   You want a drink, Esteban? Me and my brother have been kinda gettin' into Henry's bottle here a little bit.

Esteban   Oh, no, no, Mr Ray. Thank you, no. I no touch liquor no more. No more for me. (*Giggles*) Is finished. Too many beautiful women have leave me. Now – when I need them most, they are gone. And I am sober. Is funny, no?

Ray   Yeah. That is pretty funny. (*Pause.*) So, you don't drink at all? Is that the story, Esteban?

Esteban   No, sir. No more for me.

Ray   Well, my brother was just telling me you knocked one back now and then with the old man.

Esteban (*to* **Earl**)   Oh, no, Mr Earl! I pretend with Henry. Only pretend. He never notice. *Muy borracho!* (*Turns back to* **Ray**.) Long as I make the motion, you know. (*He mimes taking a drink.*) Tilt the glass; bend the elbow – that is all he cares. Just the motion. He like the company, your father. He like the human – smell.

Ray   So, you mean – that night, when the taxi came to pick him up, you were just *pretending* to drink with him? You were – (*Mimes drink.*) just pretending?

Esteban   Taxi? Oh, yes. Pretending. *Sí.* Only pretend.

Pause. **Ray** *looks at* **Earl***, then back to* **Esteban***.*

Ray   And uh – Henry just kinda went along with that, I guess, huh? He was so happy to be in your company – so starved for human companionship.

Esteban (*laughs*)   He was very drunk, Mr Ray. Very, very drunk. Like a mad dog.

Ray   And this – woman – 'Conchita' or whatever her name was – she was very drunk too? Very, very drunk?

Esteban   Conchita?

Pause. **Esteban** *turns to* **Earl***.* **Earl** *shrugs.*

Earl   I don't know. He just doesn't get the picture, Esteban. I been trying to explain it to him –

Esteban   'Conchita'? (*Laughs.*) 'Conchita', no! You mean Conchalla. Conchalla Lupina! No 'Conchita'.

Ray   Conchalla Lupina?

Esteban (*laughing*)   *Sí! Eso.*

Ray (*to* **Earl**)   Conchalla Lupina? Sounds like an opera singer.

Earl   Does kinda, doesn't it? Conchalla Lupina.

Esteban   Conchalla! She is – *magnífica*! You would not believe this woman, Mr Ray.

Ray   Is that a fact.

Esteban   She is – she is – how do you say it? Your father will tell you. She has – a big reputation down here in Bernalillo. (*Laughs.*)

Ray   Is that right? How'd she come by that?

Esteban *stops himself. He and* **Earl** *exchange looks. Pause.* **Ray** *stares at them.*

Ray   What's going on between you two? Something's going on here.

Earl   Nothing's going on.

Ray   Something's going on. What's the deal with this woman?

Esteban   Oh, Mr Ray – Conchalla is very mysterious woman. With a woman like this, believe me, a man could die in her arms and thank the saints! He could pray for no better way to leave this suffering world.

Ray   Yeah, I'd like to meet her.

Esteban   They say she has done men in like that. The lucky ones. Can you imagine something like that?

Ray   Something like what, Esteban?

Esteban   Oh, you know, Mr Ray. You know –

He begins to gyrate his pelvis and go into frantic laughter, holding his stomach, then he suddenly stops. **Ray** *stares at him.*

Esteban   Oh, I am sorry, Mr Ray – I get – when I think of her I – If you saw her you would know. She would burn a hole right through your heart! Right here! (*Stabs his chest with his fingers.*) Right through the center of your soul! Right there!

He pokes his finger hard into **Ray***'s chest, then quickly backs away. Short pause, then* **Ray** *leaps out of chair and grabs* **Esteban** *by the collar.*

Esteban   Oh – I am sorry, sir.

Ray (*shaking* **Esteban**)   What'd I tell you about that 'sir' shit! Huh? What'd I fuckin' tell you!

Ray *shoves* **Esteban** *backwards.* **Esteban** *trips back and falls to the floor.*

Earl (*going to* **Esteban**)   Hey! What is the matter with you, Ray? You gone nuts or something?

Ray   I warned him! I told him about that 'sir' stuff. I don't like the implication.

Earl (*helping* **Esteban** *to his feet, brushing him off*)   What implication? What're you talking about?

Ray   I haven't done anything to earn that kind of respect from him. That's something you say to someone you respect. He doesn't know me from Adam. How does he know I'm somebody he should respect?

Earl   Well, he knows now, doesn't he?

Ray   Yeah. Yeah! Maybe he'll think twice before going around calling strangers 'sir'. Who does he think he is, calling me 'sir'?

Earl *moves to* **Ray***, holding his finger up.*

Earl   Look, pal –

Ray   Go ahead, Earl. Poke me in the chest. I need to get poked again. Real hard. Right here!

He pokes his own chest, daring **Earl**. *Pause.* **Earl** *glares at him as* **Esteban** *stands by.*

Ray   Come on, Earl. It's been a long time, hasn't it?

Pause with the brothers staring each other down as **Esteban** *watches.* **Earl** *backs down and turns away from* **Ray**.

Earl   Look – let's just relax here, all right? How 'bout we just relax?

Ray   I am relaxed. 'Pal.'

Earl *moves to table, sits and pours himself a drink.* **Esteban** *keeps staring at* **Ray**.

Earl (*at table*)   No need to get all worked up over nothing. Things are hard enough. You gotta be careful at a time like this. I mean – How 'bout we just have a – have a drink.

Ray   He doesn't drink, remember? He *pretends* to drink. He's a pretender.

Earl   Back off, Ray! What kind of bug have you got up your ass anyway? Huh? The man comes over here with *soup*. He comes over here just as polite and neighborly as he can be and you jump all over him like a cold sweat. What is the matter with you?

Ray   Tell him to stop staring at me.

Earl   You've terrified him is what you've done.

Ray   Tell him to stop staring at me.

Earl   Come on, Esteban – (*Moves toward* **Esteban**.) Look – I apologize for my brother's behavior –

Ray   Don't apologize for me! I don't need you to apologize for my behavior! Tell him to stop staring at me.

Earl *escorts* **Esteban** *back to the table and sits him down.*

Earl   Everything's fine. Don't pay any attention to him. He – flies off the handle like this – I don't know. He – it'll be all right. Everything's fine. **Earl** *sits* **Esteban** *down, then sits in the other chair. Pause.*

Ray (*mimicking* **Earl**)   'Everything's fine.'

Pause. **Ray** *stares at them.* **Esteban** *sticks his finger in the soup.*

Earl   Everything's fine, Esteban.

Ray   Stop saying that! Stop saying that over and over again like some lame prayer! Everything's *not* fine! Everything's the opposite of 'fine'! 'Fine' is when your heart soars! When you're in love or something. That's when things are 'fine'. Right, Esteban? 'Fine' is –

Ray *suddenly stops. Long pause.* **Earl** *and* **Esteban** *stare at him.*

Ray   I wanna know about this woman.

Earl   What woman?

Ray   This woman – this mysterious woman: 'Conchalla', 'Conchita', whatever her name is.

Esteban   'Conchita.'

He starts giggling uncontrollably. Short pause.

Ray   Shut up! You shut up!

Esteban *stops abruptly. Short pause.*

Ray   Who is she, Earl?

Earl   His girlfriend. Henry's girlfriend.

Ray   Well, see now that – just confuses the hell outta me. I never even knew Henry had a girlfriend.

Earl   I told you he had a girlfriend.

Ray   You told me jack shit, Earl.

Earl   I told you on the phone.

Ray   How long's he had this 'girlfriend'? Where'd he meet her?

Earl   I don't know where he met her. (*Pause.*)

Ray   Where'd he meet her, Esteban?

Esteban   In jail.

Ray   In jail. That's cute. (*He turns to* **Earl**.)

Earl   I never met the woman, myself.

Ray   *You* never met her but Esteban here knows all about her evidently.

Earl   I heard he had a girlfriend but I never actually laid eyes on her.

Esteban   They meet in jail.

Ray   What do they have, a co-educational drunk tank down here in Bernalillo?

Esteban   They meet in jail.

Ray   That where you met her too?

Earl   Don't get personal.

Ray   Well, this is kind of a personal thing here, Earl. Girlfriends and jail. This is something different than a photograph from 1931. This is something actual here.

Earl   The man's a neighbor!

Ray   Yeah, right. Come here, neighbor! I wanna show you something.

He grabs **Esteban** *by the back of the neck, hauls him out of the chair and starts taking him toward* **Henry**'s *corpse.* **Earl** *leaps up.*

Earl   What're you doing?

Earl *grabs hold of* **Esteban**'s *arm and pulls against* **Ray**.

Ray   Come here. Now take a look at this.

Earl   Ray!

Ray *manages to swing* **Esteban** *upstage at the head of the bed with* **Earl** *still holding onto him.* **Ray** *is downstage of the bed, back to audience. He whips the sheet and blanket back, revealing* **Henry**'s *face* *to* **Esteban** *but blocking it from view of the audience.* **Esteban** *stares at the corpse.*

Ray   Go ahead – touch his face, Esteban! This is Henry. 'Mr Henry'! The man you've been bringing soup to for all these years.

Ray *grabs* **Esteban***'s hand and pushes it down onto the face of the corpse.* **Earl** *tries to pull* **Esteban** *away, but it's too late.*

Ray (*holding* **Esteban***'s hand down on corpse*) You feel how cold that is? Like ice! Like stone in a river. Does that look like a man who's ever gonna eat another bowl of soup?

Ray *releases* **Esteban***'s hand and spreads the blanket back over the corpse, covering the head completely.* **Esteban** *just stands there in shock, trembling.* **Earl** *moves slowly back toward table. Pause.*

Ray   So –

Earl (*moving toward table*)   You better get outta here, Ray.

Ray   I just got here, Earl.

Earl   There's a certain – kind of cruelty to you, isn't there? I never realized that before.

Ray   Yeah, I get mean as a snake when I don't see the whole picture.

Earl (*referring to* **Esteban**)   You had no call to be doing that to him.

Ray   What're we gonna do? Pretend?

Earl   You come waltzing in here – No idea – no concept whatsoever.

Ray   Concept?

Earl *sits at table.* **Esteban** *begins to weep softly upstage.*

Earl   Yeah. Yeah, that's right. No concept that there might be repercussions. That there might be consequences – serious consequences.

Ray (*moving toward* **Earl**)   Have you lost your tiny mind out here, Earl? Is that what happened to you? Sitting here all alone with dead Daddy for days on end. Something went on here! Didn't it, Earl? Something I'm not being let in on!

Earl   Nothing went on!

Ray   'Nothing went on.' 'Everything's fine.' (*Moves in closer to* **Earl**.) Henry was tough as an old boot! You know that. He could kill two pints and a six-pack in one sitting and never skip a beat! Now you want me to believe he takes off on a two-day binge with some Indian chippie and drops dead overnight? Is that what you're telling me?

Earl (*smashes down on table*)   It was an accumulating illness! He was a fuckin' alcoholic, Ray!

Long pause. Just the sound of **Esteban** *softly weeping.*

Ray (*to* **Esteban**)   Stop that goddamn whimpering!

Esteban *stops.*

Ray   You weren't related to him, were you?

Esteban *shakes his head, stands there trembling by* **Henry**'s *bed.*

Ray   Then what're you carrying on about? I'm his *son!* You don't see me whimpering do you?

Esteban *shakes his head.*

Ray   I've got every right to be whimpering but you don't see me doing that.

Earl   Ah, Ray, give it up.

Ray (*turning on* **Earl**)   Or you! What about you? I suppose you think you've got some sort of private thing going – some kind of special link to the corpse or something. You're in deep communion here with old Henry. (*Pause.*) Old dead Henry. (*Pause.*)

Earl   What'd you ever come out here for, Ray? Why'd you even bother?

Ray   I just couldn't believe it, I guess.

Earl   You thought he'd live for ever? Is that it?

Ray   No. I just thought –

Earl   What?

Ray   Maybe I'd see him one more time. Alive.

Earl   Yeah. You thought maybe you'd get to the bottom of something – clear things up? Make some big reconciliation.

Ray   I don't need any reconciliation! I don't need it with you either!

Earl   Good. That's good, Ray – because, guess what? It'll never happen. He's gone now.

He moves away from **Ray** *to* **Esteban**. *He puts his arm around* **Esteban**'s *shoulder and pats him, then starts leading him toward door.*

Ray   What're you doing?

Earl   We're gonna go down and make that phone call, Ray. Down to the Sonic there.

Ray   What phone call? The meat-wagon boys? So – your little period of mourning has suddenly come to an end?

Earl   Let it go, Ray! Give it up! Go on back to wherever you came from.

Pause.

Ray   No – no, I'm not gonna give it up, Earl. You know why? Because I'm your witness. I'm your little brother. I saw you, Earl. I saw the whole thing.

Earl   You saw shit.

Ray   I saw you!

Earl *takes* **Esteban** *toward door.*

Earl   Come on, Esteban.

Ray   I saw you run!

Earl *suddenly whirls around and attacks* **Ray**. *He overpowers him and sends him crashing across stage into refrigerator.* **Ray** *hits the floor.* **Earl** *crosses to him and kicks* **Ray** *in the stomach.* **Ray** *collapses.* **Esteban** *stays by door, watching. Pause as* **Earl** *straightens out his coat, then turns back to* **Esteban.** **Ray** *stays on floor.*

Earl   I'm sorry about all this, Esteban. I truly am. I hate this kind of thing, myself. Family stuff.

He moves toward **Esteban**, *then stops about halfway. He looks back at* **Ray**, *then speaks to* **Esteban.**

Earl   I had no idea my brother was so screwed up in the head like this. I mean, I knew he had some problems but I thought he'd pulled himself back together. Otherwise I'd never have called him. Anyhow – we better go make that call.

He goes to door and opens it for **Esteban.** **Esteban** *exits, then* **Earl** *turns back to* **Ray**.

Earl (*to* **Ray**, *on floor*)   Well – At least this'll give you a chance to spend a little time alone with Henry, Ray. Maybe that's what you need. Did me a world of good.

He exits, closes door behind him. Pause. **Ray** *stares at door, then hauls himself to his feet, holding his ribs. He stares at* **Henry**'s *corpse, then crosses to bed and stops with his back to audience. Pause as he stares down at corpse; then, with a quick jerk, he draws the curtain closed in front of the bed. Short pause, then lights fade quickly to black.*

Prelude to Act Two (Drunken Rhumba)

*Lights go to black. A new, more spirited mariachi piece comes up to volume. White spotlight hits **Henry** and **Conchalla** on the opposite side of the stage (extreme down right). They are still amazingly drunk and in the same tight embrace. Again they dance across the apron, doing some variations and disappear off left. Spotlight out; lights up on the set to begin Act Two.*

Act Two

*Scene: Day. Same set. The sound of rubber gloves snapping in the dark; labored breathing. Lights come up on two **Funeral Attendants** dressed in gray suits, rubber gloves, and white gauze masks covering nose and mouth. They are struggling to place **Henry**'s corpse inside a black canvas body bag. A stretcher sits on the floor downstage of the bed. They are having a great deal of difficulty getting the body to fit into the bag. They work nervously, under the constant scrutiny of **Ray**, who sits in the stage-left chair. **Taxi**, a cab driver from Albuquerque, stands upstage of the table facing audience. He is drinking from a bottle of Tiger Rose and fiddling with the tools in **Henry**'s toolbox, which is still on the table. The photo album lies open on the table where **Earl** left it. **Ray** continues to focus on the **Attendants** as **Taxi** rambles on.*

Taxi (*to* **Ray**)   Hey, look – for a hundred bucks and a bottle of Tiger Rose – are you kidding? This is gravy! This is a day off for me. I'll just regard it as that. A whole free day, thanks to you. Whatever your name is. I didn't catch the name –

*He toasts **Ray** with the bottle but **Ray** ignores him. **Attendants** continue struggling with body.*

Taxi   I mean, all the dispatcher told me is, some guy from Bernalillo wanted to talk to me. That's all the information I got. (*Pause.*) Oh, well – I was on the verge of quitting anyhow, if you wanna know the truth. Company sucks. All they care about is the damn meter. Human interest is not number one on their list. Far as they're concerned they'd just as soon have a damn robot drive the cars. Cut their insurance in half. It's coming to that. I guarandamnteeya. Computerized robot taxis. You won't even see a human being behind the wheel anymore. I'm not lyin'.

Pause. **Attendants** *keep working, making some progress, trying to zip the bag shut.* **Ray** *keeps watching them intently.* **Taxi** *drinks and picks up the large ratchet out of the toolbox – the same ratchet* **Ray** *was handling in Act One. He starts fooling with it as he talks, causing the ratchet to make a rhythmic clicking.*

Taxi   Oh, well – Thank God I'm self-sufficient. I could head on out to Norman, Oklahoma, and get me a job easy. Plenty a cabs out there. College town too. Plenty a babes. A whole slam a Miss Oklahomas have come outta Norman, lemme tell ya. I ain't lyin'. You wouldn't believe the types. Legs up to here. Asses like hard cantaloupes. Some gorgeous babes in that country. No question. I could head on out there and be in high cotton.

Pause. **Taxi** *keeps clicking the ratchet.* **Ray** *keeps staring at* **Attendants** *as they work.*

Taxi   Nice ratchet.

Ray   Don't mess with that.

Taxi   What?

Ray   I said, don't mess with that.

Taxi   Oh. Sorry. (*He puts the ratchet back in toolbox; takes another swig.*)

Ray   That doesn't belong to you.

Taxi   No – I know. I was just, uh – admiring it, that's all –

Pause. **Attendants** *keep working.*

Taxi   Were these your daddy's tools?

Ray   They're mine.

Taxi   Oh. Pretty nice. Cheap but nice.

He idly shifts to the album and starts leafing through it.

Ray (*focused on* **Attendants**)   Don't mess with that either.

Taxi   Okay. Sorry. Just – Just lookin' that's all.

Ray   Well, don't look. It's none of your business.

Taxi   Right. (*Pause.*) Well – like I was saying about, uh – Norman.

Ray   Who's Norman?

Taxi   No – I mean, uh – Norman, Oklahoma. You know – Like I was saying before about Norman, Oklahoma.

Ray   What about it?

Taxi   Well – I mean, that's what I was saying – I can go on out there and if the taxi deal doesn't work out I can always get in on the midnight pizza delivery thing. You know – late-night stuff. I've heard all about it, believe you me. Two, three in the morning sometimes, you can get a delivery call. Take a pineapple combo over to some dormitory, for instance. Well – you know who orders a pineapple combo, don't ya?

Pause. **Ray** *doesn't look at him; keeps watching* **Attendants**.

Ray   What?

Taxi   I said, you know who usually orders a pineapple combo, don't ya? Girls! That's who always orders those pineapple combos. Girls mostly. So there you are in the perfect setup! Standing there on the front stoop, ringing the bell with red pizza juice dripping down your elbow. And who comes to the door but the goddamn Miss America contest!

Henry's *body, now encased in the bag, suddenly crashes to the floor as the* **Attendants** *lose their grip.* **Ray** *stands abruptly. Everyone freezes. Pause.*

Ray   That's my father you just dropped. That's not a piece of luggage or a sack of feed! That's my father. Get out. Get outta here.

Attendants *exit.*

Taxi   They don't care. They're just hauling stiffs. They've seen it a thousand times. A corpse is a corpse. Might as well be roadkill to them.

Ray   Shut up.

Taxi   You need some help with that?

Ray *motions 'no'. Goes to door and calls back the* **Attendants**.

Ray   You guys come back. Both of you come back in here.

Attendants *re-enter and lift* **Henry**'s *body again, struggling with the weight as* **Ray** *slowly closes in on them.* **Taxi** *stays where he is.*

Ray   You aren't the type of creeps who make sick jokes behind other people's backs are you? Because if you are I'll find out about it and I'll seek vengeance on your heads.

Pause.

Now get outta here.

The **Attendants** *hustle the corpse out the door and disappear.* **Ray** *stays in open doorway looking offstage, after them.* **Taxi** *stays at the table with album.*

Taxi *(laughing, still going through album)*   That's good! That's good! 'I'll seek vengeance on your heads!' That's a good one. Where'd you come up with that? I'll have to remember that. I can use that. That has a kinda – old-fashioned ring to it. You know, like – King Arthur or something? Remember him?

Ray *closes door and turns to* **Taxi**. *Pause. They stare at each other.*

Ray   What'd I tell you about that album?

Taxi   What? *(He quickly looks back at album)* Oh – *(He shuts album.)* Sorry. I forgot.

Pause. **Ray** *moves to* **Henry**'s *empty bed. He stares at bed, then smooths the blanket and sheet. He draws the curtain closed in front of bed and just stands there staring at curtain with his back to* **Taxi**. *Pause. Stays by table.*

Taxi   Well – anyhow, I appreciate the hundred bucks and the Tiger Rose. I surely do. Came as a complete surprise to me when the dispatcher gave me the message. Not that I don't deserve it. (*Laughs.*) I deserve every bit of it. You better believe it!

Pause. **Ray** *doesn't move, just keeps staring at the bed with his back to* **Taxi**.

Taxi   How'd you track me down, anyhow? That's a big mystery. I couldn't figure that one out. I mean it's been almost a week ago I was out here. Least a week, wasn't it? I lose track.

Pause. **Ray** *doesn't move. Silence.*

Taxi   Well, anyhow, I suppose this is a hard time for you, huh? I mean, I don't mind answering any questions you might have. You said you had some questions. Not that I could tell you much –

Pause. **Ray** *turns to him and stares, then moves downstage to table and sits; pours himself a drink.* **Taxi** *slowly pulls out a chair, as though to sit down at the table.*

Ray (*cold*)   Don't sit down at this table.

Taxi *freezes, then stands and pushes chair back in place. Pause.*

Ray   I don't know you well enough for you to be sitting at this table.

Taxi   Right. Uh – sorry. I was thinking maybe if I sat at the table – we could uh – we could get to know each other – a little – maybe. You know – break the ice. (*Laughs.*)

Ray   What makes you think I want to get to know you? I didn't pay you to come all the way out here so I could get to know you. What do you think you are?

Taxi   Me? Well – I'm –

Ray   Go over and stand by the door.

Taxi   What?

Pause. **Taxi** *looks toward the door, then back to* **Ray**, *but doesn't move.*

Ray (*pointing to door*)   Over there.

Taxi *looks to the door again, then back to* **Ray**.

Taxi   Now, you mean?

Ray   Yeah. Now. When you're a stranger in somebody's house, you don't automatically assume you can sit down at their table and fool around aimlessly with their father's possessions.

Taxi   I thought they were yours. You told me –

Ray   Go over and stand by the door!

Taxi *looks at door again, then back to* **Ray**. *Pause, then he crosses to door, taking his bottle with him, and stands there. He stares at* **Ray**.

Taxi   Right here?

Ray   A little to your right. (**Taxi** *adjusts his position slightly.*)

Taxi   How's this?

Ray   That's good. Now stay right there. Okay?

Taxi   Okay. (*Takes a drink from his bottle.*) Sure. You bet.

Ray   Don't move from that spot.

Taxi   Okay.

Ray   See if you can manage that. Now, just for a minute, try to avoid thinking of yourself as anything special. All right? Anything out of the ordinary. You're nothing. Just like me. An empty nothing. A couple of nothings whose lives have never amounted to anything and never will. Do you think you can go along with this?

Taxi   Well, I don't know. I mean – it's not exactly the way I was raised. My uncle used to –

Ray   I'm not interested in the way you were raised, or your uncle.

Taxi   Right.

Ray   I'm not interested in Norman, Oklahoma, or 'babes' or pizza juice dripping down your arm or your employment problems either.

Taxi   Right.

Ray   I'm only interested in one thing.

Taxi (*pause*)   What's that?

Ray   What happened that night you showed up here in your cab to take my father out to go fishing? What exactly happened?

Pause.

Taxi   Oh. Well – I don't know. Nothin' special. I mean, I got the call. You know, it was kinda unusual but –

He starts to move toward **Ray**.

Ray   Just stay by the door!

Taxi *freezes, then returns to his spot by the door. Pause. He takes another drink from his bottle.*

Taxi   Right here?

Ray   A little to your left. (**Taxi** *adjusts his position.*) That's fine. Now – you were saying – it was unusual?

Taxi   Yeah.

Ray   Kind of unusual but not all that unusual.

Taxi (*stays put*)   No, right. I mean – we get calls now and then from folks way out in the boondocks like this. This is big country – lotta ground between places. Folks need a ride. Stranded folks. I mean, I remember as a kid we grew up a hundred and twenty miles from the nearest drive-in.

Ray   Don't get off the subject.

Pause.

Taxi   What?

Ray   Your mind is wandering. Don't allow it to do that.

Taxi   Oh – yeah – well – like I was saying – all I do is drive
'em to the nearest movie. Forty, fifty miles maybe sometimes.
Just to see Clint Eastwood.

Ray   You arrived here at the house! Right? I don't care how
long it took you to get here. You arrived. Now, what was going
on here at the house when you arrived?

Taxi   Here?

Ray   Yeah. That's right. Here.

Taxi   Oh. Well – nothing really. I mean – I remember
knocking. I remember this feeling like – maybe I was at the
wrong house or something.

Ray   Why was that?

*Lights slowly shift. A glowing amber light comes up on the curtain in front
of* **Henry**'s *bed. At the same time the lights on the rest of the stage dim
to a pale moonlit glow.*

Taxi   Well, I mean – there wasn't any answer at the door.
I kept knocking and –

He moves slowly toward the curtain and the bed as **Ray** *turns slowly in
his chair until he's directly facing the audience.* **Ray** *stays in this position,
looking directly out at the audience through the entire flashback.*

Taxi (*as he crosses to curtain in front of bed*) I could hear something
from inside so I knew there was somebody in here. I kept
knocking but all I heard was this moaning like – this weeping.
I didn't know what to make of it. Door was open so – I just let
myself in. And there he was – lying on his side in bed there.
Sobbing like –

The curtain opens slowly on its own, revealing the living **Henry**, *lying
on his belly, softly weeping.* **Taxi** *approaches him.*

Taxi (*to* **Henry**) Mr Moss? (*Pause.*) Mr Moss?

Henry *suddenly sits up on the edge of the bed with a jerk and stares
blankly at* **Taxi**. *He stops weeping. Pause. He gets up fast and snatches
the bottle of Tiger Rose away from* **Taxi**, *then crosses to the door,
staggering slightly.*

Henry (*crossing to door*)   The hell you doin' with my bottle! The fuck is this? Time is it, anyway?

Henry *opens the door, looks out, then slams it shut. He turns to* **Taxi** *and stares at him.*

Taxi   Did you – call a cab, Mr Moss?

Henry   A what?

Taxi   A taxi. From Albuquerque? Verde Cabs?

Henry   Taxi? The fuck is this? A taxi from Albuquerque?

Taxi   Somebody called a cab.

Henry   Somebody?

Taxi   Somebody must have.

Henry   What if they did? Maybe they did, maybe they didn't. What's the big deal?

He crosses to the table and sits in the upstage chair, ignoring **Ray**, *as though* **Ray** *didn't exist.* **Henry** *drinks from* **Taxi**'s *bottle.*

Henry (*looking at bottle*)   The fuck is this junk? (*Pushes bottle on table.*) Where'd this come from?

Taxi   I'm the taxi.

Henry   What?

Taxi   I'm the taxi from Albuquerque.

Henry (*laughs*)   You're the taxi? That's something! You look like a damn taxi. You got that yellow stripe down your back.

He grabs bottle back and drinks, then gags on it.

What the hell is this stuff anyhow?

Taxi   Tiger Rose.

Henry   Stuff stinks! (*Pushes bottle away again.*) That's not my stuff. Where the hell's my stuff?

He stands and starts wandering around looking for his bottle.

Taxi   Did you wanna go somewhere, Mr Moss? Did you want me to take you somewhere?

Henry (*searching*)   I had a bottle here. You didn't walk off with my damn bottle, did ya?

Taxi   No, sir, I just got here.

Henry   Well, somebody's got my bottle!

Taxi   Mr Moss, did you need me to take you somewhere? That's what I'm here for. I'm here to take you wherever you want to go.

Henry (*stops, looks at* **Taxi**)   You're here to take me?

Taxi   That's right.

Henry   Where do I wanna go?

Taxi   Well – that's what I'm here to find out – I mean –

Henry   Where could it be that I wanna go?

Taxi   I have no idea, sir.

Henry   What the hell happened to that bottle?

He starts searching for bottle again.

Taxi   Maybe that was it, huh? Maybe you needed me to take you to get a bottle?

Henry   That's what you think. That's probably what you think! Do I look that desperate to you?

Taxi   No, sir.

Henry   You lyin' sack a doggy doo-doo.

Taxi   I'm going to have to go, Mr Moss.

He makes a move to leave. **Henry** *stops him.*

Henry   Just a second, just a second, just a second! Just hold on here. You're the taxi, right?

Taxi   That's right. Yeah.

Henry   And you've got a mission. Is that it? You were called to come here?

Taxi   Yes, sir.

Henry   So somebody musta called you out here. Is that correct?

Taxi   Yeah. That's correct.

Henry   And you think that was me who called you out here?

Taxi   Well – I don't know who it was, but –

Henry   Well, it was me. Why beat around the bush about it?

Taxi   It was you?

Henry   'Course it was. You don't see anybody else around here, do ya?

Taxi   Well, I'm ready, Mr Moss.

Henry   Yeah, yeah, yeah. You're ready. You're ready. Sure. You're always ready. Suppose you got the meter runnin' out there too, huh? Rackin' it up for air time! Click-clocking away!

Taxi   Well, the company says you gotta –

Henry   Fuck the company, all right! Fuck the company right where it fits. What're you, a company man? Is that what you are?

Taxi   No, sir, I'm –

Henry   Are you a company man or are you your own man? That's the question. What is it? You can't have it both ways.

Taxi   I'm my own –

Henry   You don't have a clue, buster.

Taxi   I just need some kind of insurance that you actually want the cab –

Henry   Insurance! Money, you mean? Cash money? That's what you're worried about?

Taxi No, I –

Henry *starts digging cash out of his pockets. He crosses to table and slams it down.*

Henry Cash money! Mean green! How 'bout that! Look at that! Where would a desperate man come up with so much cash! Surprised ya, huh? Give ya a start?

Taxi No, sir.

Henry That's blood money right there, Mr Taxi! World War Two blood money! Guess how many dead Japs that cost? Take a guess.

Taxi I, uh –

Henry Beyond your imagination, bud. Beyond your imagination.

Taxi Well, I didn't think you didn't have any money, Mr Moss. That wasn't what I meant.

Henry You got any women, Taxi?

Pause. **Taxi** *stares at him.*

Taxi Women? You mean –

Henry I mean, women. The female kind.

Taxi Well, I've got a girlfriend, if that's what you mean.

Henry Girlfriend? Don't gimme that shit. 'Girlfriend.' I mean women. Women women. Real women!

Taxi Well – she's real, all right.

Henry I got one. I got a doozy. Make yer tail swim, Taxi. Know what she did to me? You wanna know? Guess. Bet you'll never guess.

Taxi Mr Moss, I gotta –

Henry She pronounced me dead! That's what she did. (*Pause.*)

Taxi   Dead?

Henry   That's it. Dead. Ever heard of such a thing? That's what she did to me. Can you imagine? Right in jail too. In front of everyone. We were both incarcerated together and she made that pronouncement. Publicly! Standing right over my semi-conscious body. She just bellowed it out to the general jail community at large. 'Señor Moss is dead!' Now it's all over town. All over this territory. Everyone thinks I'm dead!

Pause. **Henry** *grabs bottle again; drinks.* **Taxi** *just stands there.*

Taxi   Well – they must know she was lying by now, don't they?

Henry   On the contrary! Nobody thinks she was lying. Not a single solitary soul.

Taxi   Well – I mean – You're not dead, so –

Henry   You think I'm not dead. That's you. But you're not from around here, are you?

Taxi   No, sir, but –

Henry   You're from Albuquerque.

Taxi   Yes, sir.

Henry   So what difference does it make what you think? I'm talkin' about the ones right around here. The real ones. They're all that count. All the local ones. I'm a well-known figure around here, in case you didn't know that, buster. They all think I'm dead now on account a her.

Taxi   Well, don't they see you walking around and talking and everything?

Henry   Walking around and talking? What the hell difference does that make? There's a whole shitload of 'walkers' and 'talkers' – fabricating and perambulating their butts off! You think they're all in the land of the living? Is that what you think? Huh?

Taxi   I know, but usually –

Henry   Usually nothin'! There's nothin' usual about this! I'm in a serious jam on account of this woman! She's trying to obliterate me before my natural time! She took out an obituary in the paper. 'Henry Jamison Moss. Dead. Deceased. Causes unknown.' She did that to me.

Taxi   Well, can't you just explain to everyone that she was mistaken?

Henry   What's the situation look like to you, bub? Do I look like a dead man or what?

Taxi   No, sir.

Henry   Not the least bit, huh? Not around the eyes a little? Look around the eyes. That's what gives it away. Look closely here. Come over and give it a good hard look-see.

Taxi *reluctantly approaches* **Henry** *and stops in front of him, staring hard at* **Henry***'s eyes.*

Henry   No, you've got to get in here close! Scrutinize this. Penetrate past the outer covering.

Taxi *moves in closer and bends in toward* **Henry***'s face, staring hard at his eyes.* **Henry** *opens his eyes wide, using his fingers and thumbs to pry them open.*

Henry   Now – look right deep into the pupil, where it's dark. Where it drops off into nowhere. You see that? Right straight in there like you were riding a train into a black tunnel. What do you see? Tell me what you see.

Pause. **Taxi** *stares hard into* **Henry***'s eyes.*

Taxi   Nothing.

Henry *drops his hands from his eyes.*

Henry   Exactly! Exactly my point. Absolutely nothing!

Taxi   No, I mean, they look okay to me.

Henry   They look dead!

Taxi   No, sir –

Henry   Don't jerk my chain, Taxi-man! You're a lyin' dog! Yer from Albuquerque!

Taxi *backs off from* **Henry**.

Taxi   Are you ready to go someplace, Mr Moss, because – I've gotta head on back if you don't need the cab.

Henry *moves in front of him fast and stops him.*

Henry   Not so fast, not so fast, not so fast!

Taxi   I can't be just – hanging around here, Mr Moss. There's other customers waiting.

Pause. **Henry** *pats* **Taxi** *on the shoulder.*

Henry   So – just from your – casual observation, you think there might be a little spark inside there, huh? (*Pointing to his eyes.*) A little ember of hope?

Taxi   You're not dead, all right! As far as I can tell you are not dead!

Pause.

Henry   Good, that's good. That's the first positive note I've heard in months. Tell ya what we're gonna do – Tell ya what, Taxi. Here's what we're gonna do – Ya like to trout fish?

Taxi   Well – sure. Haven't done it in a while, but –

Henry   Well, that's what we're gonna do, then. Conchalla likes to trout fish too. We're gonna go pick her up and hit the river. You can take it up with her.

Taxi   Conchalla?

Henry   That's right. Conchalla Lupina. That's the woman. The woman I was referring to. You can take the whole issue up with her out on the Pecos.

He grabs **Taxi** *by the shoulder and starts to weave toward the door.*

Taxi   What issue?

Henry   The question of my being! My aliveness! My actuality in this world! Whether or not I'm dead or not! What the hell've we been talkin' about here? Pay attention to the subject!

Taxi   But, I'm not –

Henry   Just get that cab fired up, bub! Get those pistons rockin'! You'll see. Conchalla's a very influential woman around here. Sharp as jailhouse coffee. You can have it out with her, toe to toe. You can argue my case for me. I've got no one else. Couple a lamebrain sons who couldn't find their peckers in a pickle jar. Take hold of my arm now, boy. Take ahold! (**Taxi** *grabs* **Henry**'s *arm.*) That feel like a living arm to you?

Taxi   Yes, sir. It does.

Henry   Attaboy! You tell her that for me. She might just listen to an outsider from Albuquerque. She might just listen.

He staggers out through door and disappears, leaving **Taxi** *behind.* **Taxi** *closes door and turns to face* **Ray**, *who remains seated, facing audience. Lights return to previous setup.* **Ray** *takes a drink. Pause. He keeps staring out at audience with his back to* **Taxi**.

Ray   That's it? That's all you can remember?

Taxi (*stays by door*)   That's pretty much it. Yeah.

Ray   No more details?

Taxi   Details? Like what?

Ray   Are you still on your spot? Your same spot?

Taxi   What spot?

Ray   Your spot by the door where I told you to stay.

Taxi (*adjusting*)   Oh – yeah. Yeah, I'm still there.

He jumps into position. Pause.

Ray   Good. That's very good.

Pause. **Ray** *gets up from chair and crosses to* **Henry**'s *bed. He sits on bed, facing audience. Pause.*

Taxi   Look – why don't I just give you the hundred bucks back, okay?

He digs in his pocket and pulls out money.

I'll keep the Tiger Rose and we'll call it even-steven. Just for the trip out here. Gas and time involved. We'll write that off. How's that sound?

Ray (*laughs*)   'Even-steven'?

Pause. **Ray** *goes silent.* **Taxi** *moves very cautiously toward* **Ray**, *holding out the money to him.*

Taxi   That sound fair to you? I mean – I don't think this is gonna work out, personally. I just got a feeling – I mean, I had a whole different idea about this. Here. (*Offering money to* **Ray**.) How about it?

Ray   You keep that money, Taxi-man. That's your money. You put it back in your pocket. I don't want it. You put it in your pocket and go back to the door, like I told you, and stay there. All right?

Taxi   Oh no –

Ray   Go back to the door.

Pause. **Taxi** *slowly puts money back in his pocket, returns to his spot by the door and stands there. He stares at* **Ray**, *trembling slightly. Pause.* **Ray** *stares out.*

Taxi   Thing I'm gonna do is go back to Texas. Never shoulda left Texas in the first place. That's the whole problem, right there. I don't fit up here in this country. You get raised up in a friendly place, you think the whole rest of the world's just as friendly. Boy, are you sadly mistaken.

Ray *stands slowly from bed and moves to refrigerator.* **Taxi** *stays.*

Ray   You're not from Texas. You're from Albuquerque.

Taxi   I'm originally from Texas. Tyler, Texas – born and raised.

Ray *opens refrigerator and stares into it.*

Ray   Texans don't whine. No whiners down in Texas. They kicked 'em all out.

Taxi   What do you know about it? My great-great-grandmother was slaughtered by Comanches. I guess that makes me from Texas, all right.

Ray (*looking in fridge*)   Your great-great-grandmother?

Taxi   That's right.

Ray   Your great-great-grandmother was slaughtered by Comanches? Sounds like a story to me.

Taxi   A story?

Ray   A fabrication, passed down from one generation to another. Sounds like that kind of a story. A prideful story.

Taxi   Prideful? There's nothin' prideful about being slaughtered.

Ray *takes out the jar of jalapeños and slams refrigerator door shut. He opens jar, takes out a pepper, pops it in his mouth, then crosses slowly toward* **Taxi** *with the jar.* **Taxi** *stays.*

Ray (*slowly crossing to* **Taxi**)   Thing about that kind of a story, Taxi-man, is that the very first fabricator – the original liar who started this little rumor about your slaughtered great-great-grandma – he's dead and gone now, right? Vanished from this earth! All the ones who knew him are dead and gone. All that's left is a cracked tintype, maybe; a gnarly lock of bloody hair; some fingernail clippings in a leather pouch. So there's really no way to verify this little story of yours, is there? This little history.

Pause. **Ray** *stops very close to* **Taxi**'s *face, chewing on the pepper.*

Taxi   You're not calling me a liar, are you?

Ray   Your whole family's a pack of liars. They were born liars. They couldn't help themselves. That's why it's important to try to get at the heart of things, don't you think? Somebody, somewhere along the line has to try to get at the heart of things.

Pause. They stare at each other, then **Ray** *offers jar of peppers out to* **Taxi**.

Ray   Jalapeño?

Taxi   No. Thank you.

Ray   Come on, now! You're from Texas! You can take a little heat.

He slowly takes out a Jalapeño and pushes it into **Taxi***'s mouth.* **Taxi** *chews.* **Ray** *moves away from him to table and sits.* **Taxi** *starts quietly choking on pepper, eyes watering, breaking out in a sweat. He wants to grab the bottle off the table to cool the fire but is afraid to move from his spot.*

Ray (*seated at table*) No way to verify this story at all. It's like my brother. Just like my brother. He's a fabricator too. He makes something up out of thin air, thinking I'll fall for it. Just swallow it whole. No questions. 'Dad's dead.' That's how he put it. 'Dad's dead.' Simple as that. End of issue.

Taxi (*choking, gasping for air*)   Could – could I – could I get my bottle, please? Do you think –

Pause. **Ray** *stares at him as he chokes, then slides bottle in* **Taxi***'s direction.* **Taxi** *hesitates to leave his spot, but* **Ray** *gestures for him to go ahead and take bottle.* **Taxi** *lunges for bottle, takes a huge swig, clears his throat and stares at* **Ray***, his eyes popping from the heat.*

Taxi   Thanks.

Ray   You go back over to your spot now, Taxi.

Taxi   Oh, no. Couldn't we – just be friendly?

Ray   You just go on back over there. You remember where it is, don't you?

Taxi   What? My – my – spot?

Ray   Yeah.

Pause. **Taxi** *moves back to his spot by door; turns to* **Ray**.

Taxi   Was this it?

Ray Close enough.

Taxi Look – I've got this terrible feeling all of a sudden. I –
I mean I – I don't know anything. I didn't think there was
anything wrong here to begin with. I mean when I first came
over, you know. I wouldn't have volunteered for this if I thought
there was anything wrong here. I just – I don't – I gotta go
now. I really gotta go –

He moves to door as though to exit. **Ray** *suddenly flies at him from
the chair and pins him up against the door.* **Ray** *grabs him by the chest.*
Taxi *offers no resistance, just whimpers.*

Ray (*close to* **Taxi**'s *face*)   I didn't give you a hundred bucks
and a bottle of Tiger Rose so you could skip out on me!
What'd you think this was, a free ride? Huh! Is that what you
thought?

Taxi I don't want the hundred bucks! I told you that!

Ray You took it! It's too late now. You owe me. You're in
debt to me. You're deeply in debt!

Taxi Oh, my God! Oh, my God in Heaven.

Pause. **Ray** *lets go of him and backs off slowly but stands near him.*
Taxi *slumps back against door; his head bows like he's on the verge of
breaking down. He trembles all over.*

Taxi I need to get back and see my girlfriend!

Ray You don't have a girlfriend.

Taxi I do! I do too! I do so have a girlfriend! I'm from Texas
and I've got a girlfriend! How come you're trying to take
everything away from me? I don't wanna be here! I don't
wanna be here at all! I want – I wanna leave now! I wanna go!

Ray Yeah, but you owe me something now, Taxi. You owe
me a little story.

Taxi What story?

Ray The story of when you all returned; the returning story.
When you came back here. To this place, right here. With my
dad and this woman and a string of fish.

Short pause, then **Conchalla** *bursts through the door, knocking* **Taxi** *toward the bed.* **Henry** *stumbles through, close behind her, holding up a very small fish by the tail.* **Ray** *moves extreme downstage right and stands, facing audience throughout flashback. The other characters ignore him.* **Taxi** *falls in with* **Henry** *and* **Conchalla** *as an active member of the flashback.* **Conchalla** *is extremely drunk and singing loudly in some strange dialect that sounds like a mixture of Spanish and Indian. She carries a bottle of tequila and heads straight for the tub, pushing* **Taxi** *out of her way. She turns the hot water on full blast and starts taking her skirt and blouse off as she continues to sing.* **Henry** *stumbles to the table, as drunk as* **Conchalla***, and flops the fish down on it. He picks the fish up and starts flopping it back and forth on the table as he sings in competition with* **Conchalla***.*

Henry (*singing loudly:*)
  Gonna tie my pecker to a tree, to a tree.
  Gonna tie my pecker to a tree.
  Gonna tie my pecker to a tree, to a tree.
  Gonna tie my pecker to a tree.

Pause as **Henry** *looks around the room, ignoring* **Ray***.* **Conchalla** *goes into humming her song and continues getting ready for her bath. She drinks from bottle, takes some kind of oil out of her belt and starts oiling her skin as the water steams in the tub.* **Taxi** *looks on.*

Henry   Look at this fish! Now, that's a fish!

He holds the tiny fish up as though it were a trophy. **Conchalla** *laughs.*

Conchalla   That is no fish! That is a fish wishing to become a fish. A wish-fish!

Henry (*turning toward* **Conchalla***, weaving*)   I knew – I just knew – Now, how did I know that you were gonna rain on my rainbow like that? How'd I know that?

Conchalla   That is a minnow! That is a bait-fish, maybe.

Henry (*holding up fish*)   That's a legitimate fish right there! Wouldn't you say that was a legitimate fish, Taxi? That's a fish!

Taxi   Well, yeah – it's a fish but – you probably shoulda let him grow some.

Henry Let him grow? What the hell good's that? Let him grow! Ya mean throw him back is what ya mean. That's what ya mean, isn't it? Throw him back. (*To* **Conchalla**.) He wants me to throw back my catch of the day.

Conchalla That is no fish. Dead men cannot catch fish. Dead men have no need to fish. They are never hungry.

She starts laughing and climbs into the steaming tub.

Henry Don't start that up again with me! There she goes! There she goes again!

Taxi Mr Moss, I was wondering if maybe you could pay me for the trip now and I could –

Henry *ignores* **Taxi**. *He takes fish over to* **Conchalla** *in the tub and starts waving it in her face as* **Conchalla** *bathes.*

Henry She just refuses to recognize the simple truth of the thing. This is a genuine fish! A trophy fish! Look at the size of this fish!

Conchalla I remember he bragged the same way about his penis.

Henry I never bragged about my penis! That's an outright lie! I never did that. (*To* **Taxi**.) She's lying again. Look at this fish!

Conchalla That is a silly fish. That is a silly, silly fish.

She suddenly snatches the fish out of **Henry**'s *grasp and flips it into the steaming water of the tub.*

Henry (*to* **Taxi**) Did you see that? Did you see what she did?

Taxi Mr Moss, I gotta get back to my girlfriend. I mean she's –

Henry She just threw my fish into the steaming water! My one and only fish!

Conchalla There was no fish. You must have been dreaming!

Henry There was a fish! Everyone knows there was a fish!

He makes a move toward **Conchalla** *to retrieve his fish.*

Conchalla (*fierce; her voice drops an octave*)   Don't you come near this fish!

Henry *freezes.*

Conchalla   I have it between my thighs now.

Henry   Oh, she's disgusting.

Conchalla   Do you want it to come back to life?

Henry   No! I don't want it to come back to life! I caught it! It's dead. I want it to stay dead.

Conchalla   I can bring it back to life for you. It is easy.

Henry   I don't want it brought back to life! I'm gonna fry it up.

Conchalla   I just squeeze him a little between my legs. Like this –

Henry   No!

Taxi   Mr Moss, do you think we might be able to settle up here now? I need to get my money! I don't know how many times I gotta tell you.

Henry   You'll get yer damn money! Not that you deserve it. What've you been doin' fer yer money? Huh? Sittin' around choking yer chicken! That's about it. Watching her continue to insult and berate me up one side of the river and down the other. Not once did you ever make so much as a gesture on my behalf! Not once!

Taxi   I'm a driver! I'm a taxicab driver! That's what I do. I drive people around from one place to another. That's all I do. I don't know about anything else. I don't know what you expect from me.

Henry   I expect you to make a stand! That's what I expect. I've expected it all along! You told me you saw something in here. (*Points to his eyes.*) Something glimmering.

Taxi   I never said I saw something glimmering!

Henry   That's what you said.

Taxi   I never said that!

Henry   What'd you say, then?

Taxi   I said I saw nothing! Zero! Goose eggs. Absolutely nothing. It looked like a plain old everyday eyeball to me.

Henry   I'm surrounded by liars! She says there's no fish, then there is a fish.

Conchalla (*laughs, looks down between her legs*)   It's starting to swim now.

Henry   It can't be! It's dead.

He moves toward **Conchalla**, *but she stops him with a gesture.*

Conchalla (*looking down at fish*)   Come take a look at your fish. It's peaceful now. It's happy. It has found its place in this world. Look at it swimming. Swimming, swimming.

Pause.

Taxi   Mr Moss, look – If you're not going to give me the money – I mean – just tell me what you want me to do. Just tell me and I'll do it. Okay? Then you can pay me and I'll get outta here. How's that sound? What exactly is it that you wanna convince her of?

Henry   You ever been with a woman who thought you were dead?

Taxi   Well, no – I guess not. No.

Henry   Then you don't know what it's like, do ya?

Taxi   No sir, but – I mean, there must've been a time when she thought you were alive. Right?

Henry   I can't remember.

Taxi   Well – think back. Maybe if you could remember, then I could try to remind her.

Henry   Remind her of what?

Taxi   Whatever it was. Was it your walk or something?

Henry   My walk?

Taxi   Your talk?

Henry   My talk?

Taxi   Well, I don't know – Was it your smile, maybe?

Henry (*pushes* **Taxi** *away*)   Don't be an idiot!

Taxi   I'm just trying to help, is all!

Henry   You're not trying to help! All you care about is your money! Your lousy money!

Taxi   I don't know exactly what it is you want me to do.

Henry   Here's what I want you to do. Walk right over to her. Go ahead. Walk right over there to her, like a man, and explain the situation.

Taxi   What situation?

Henry   What is the matter with you?

Taxi   You mean, explain to her that you're not dead?

Henry   That's the ticket!

Taxi   How come you don't know that you're not dead? I don't get that.

Henry   I know that I'm not dead! She's the one who doesn't know that I'm not dead! Now get on over there! Just take the plunge.

Pause. **Taxi** *very tentatively approaches* **Conchalla** *as she hums softly in the tub, oblivious to the others.* **Taxi** *stops.* **Taxi** *inches closer to* **Conchalla***, who has her eyes closed, head resting back against the tub, very peacefully.*

Taxi   Uh – Miss Lupina?

No response from **Conchalla***. She just smiles, keeps her eyes closed and hums softly.*

Taxi   Uh – ma'am – you don't really know me but – I'm –
I'm the type a guy who calls a spade a spade. You know? I mean,
I'm a pretty levelheaded, honest type a guy and –

Henry   She doesn't give a shit what type a guy you are!
You're supposed to be telling her about me! What about me?

Taxi   I was getting to that. I was just – uh – Miss Lupina –
There are certain signs of life that I think we can all agree on,
aren't there? I mean, when you see someone breathing and –
yelling and –

Henry   Breathing and yelling? Breathing and yelling!

Taxi (*to* **Henry**)   Yeah! Yeah, I mean, that's what you're
doing! You're breathing and yelling so –

Henry   That's not what I wanna be known for – Breathing
and yelling! What the hell is that! I've got lots of qualities
besides breathing and yelling! Tell her about those!

Taxi   I haven't seen those.

Suddenly **Conchalla** *lets out a gasp and raises her arm up out of the
water with the fish dangling from her fingers. The fish is alive and
twitching. She raises the fish directly over her head. Her eyes open, her
mouth opens wide. Short pause, then she lets the fish drop directly into her
mouth. Her jaws close as she grinds the fish between her teeth. Her arm
drops with a mighty splash. Her eyes close again. She smiles as she goes
on chewing the fish.* **Taxi** *runs toward the door, in terror.* **Henry** *storms
toward* **Conchalla***, but she remains undisturbed.*

Henry (*to* **Conchalla**)   That was my fish she just ate!

Taxi (*by door*)   All right! That's it! That's it – I'm leaving! This
is not good for me! My girlfriend would not like me to be here
with you people! She warned me about people like you.

Suddenly the door swings open, almost knocking **Taxi** *over.* **Esteban**
stands there in doorway with another bowl of steaming soup. Pause.

Henry (*to* **Esteban**)   What the hell're you doing here?

Esteban (*smiling*)   Mr Henry, I brought you some soup.

Henry   I don't want any goddamn soup now! What're you doin', barging in here with soup? Can't you see we're busy! We're busy here!

Esteban (*still in doorway*)   I saw the taxi and – I came over. I was worried for you.

Conchalla (*from tub*)   Don't worry for the dead! Worry for the living!

Esteban   Oh – she is here? Conchalla is here?

Esteban *gets very excited and steps into the room, looking toward* **Conchalla***.*

Henry   Yeah, she's here! She ate my fish!

Conchalla *cackles and splashes in the tub.* **Esteban** *heads toward her, slowly, carrying the soup in front of him.*

Esteban   I would have brought two bowls of soup. I did not know she was here.

Conchalla   Dead men can't eat soup!

Henry (*to* **Conchalla**)   Shut up with that!

Taxi   Mr Moss, I'm asking you for the last time for my money. Ninety-six dollars and forty-two cents. That's what you owe me.

Henry *starts pulling out crumpled, wet bills from his pockets and handing them over to* **Taxi** *as he speaks.* **Esteban** *keeps heading toward* **Conchalla***, completely enraptured with her presence.* **Conchalla** *trickles water down her arms and sings to herself softly.*

Henry   All right, all right, all right! Stop whimpering about yer damn money.

Esteban   If only I had known you were here. I would have made my *carne asada.*

Henry (*as he hands over money to* **Taxi**)   What did I ever do to deserve this? I've led an honorable life for the most part. I've served my country. I've dropped bombs on total strangers! I've worked my ass off for idiots. Paid my taxes. There's never once been any question of my − existence! Never once. It's humiliating! A man my age − to be forced into this kind of position. I'm too old to be having to prove I'm alive!

Conchalla (*laughing, sing-song*)   No one will come to his rescue! No one will come to his rescue.

Esteban   The voice of an angel.

Henry *now seems to be talking to himself more than anyone else; staggering around, still doling out money to **Taxi**, who keeps counting it and asking for more. **Esteban** becomes more and more hypnotized by* **Conchalla***.*

Henry   It's true − Maybe it's true − Maybe I am on the dark side of the moon now. It's possible. Maybe I am just − just completely − gone.

Henry *appeals to **Esteban**, but **Esteban** is locked onto* **Conchalla** *with his eyes. **Taxi** only wants the money. Suddenly **Earl** appears in the open doorway, extremely drunk. **Henry** freezes and stares at him. **Ray** immediately reacts to **Earl**'s presence but still remains outside the action. He turns to face **Earl**, but **Earl** ignores him. Short pause as **Earl** just stands there, weaving slightly in doorway. **Conchalla** becomes alarmed at **Earl**'s presence. She stands in the tub and yells at* **Esteban***, who immediately reacts.*

Conchalla   Get me my blanket! I need my blanket now! No one can even take a bath in peace.

Esteban *sets down the soup, rushes to the bed, pulls the blanket off it, then takes it to* **Conchalla***, who snatches it away from him and wraps herself up in it. She stays standing in tub. **Henry** staggers toward* **Earl***.*

Henry (*to **Earl***)   What the hell're you doing, standing in my doorway? Who're you supposed to be?

Earl   I'm supposed to be your oldest son. That's who I'm supposed to be.

Henry (*turning to **Esteban***)   What is this? What's going on here?

Esteban   I called him, Mr Henry. I did not know what to do.

Henry (*approaching* **Esteban**)   You called him?

Esteban   I was worried something bad might have happened to you.

Henry   Something bad? Something bad has just happened to me. Something bad is happening to me. Treachery from every angle! Sons! Neighbors! Women! Family! There's no end to it! How's a man supposed to breathe?

Taxi *exits and closes door behind him. Then the door closes, suddenly everyone freezes except* **Ray**, *who slowly crosses over to* **Earl** *and stops right in front of him, very close. He stares at* **Earl**, *then slowly reaches out and opens* **Earl**'s *eyes very wide with his fingers and thumbs. This gesture should be reminiscent of* **Henry** *opening his eyes wide for* **Taxi** *to examine. Pause.*

Ray   I see you, Earl. I see you now.

Lights fade fast to black.

Act Three

Scene: Next morning. Same set. The photo album and tool chest are gone.
Esteban *is cooking menudo in a black pot on the stove. He has his spices and herbs, and wears an orange apron. He is very meticulous and attentive to his cooking.* **Earl** *has a raging hangover. He lies on his back on* **Henry***'s bed, holding his head with both hands and writhing with pain. He moans and tries, with no effect, to kick his boots off.* **Esteban** *hums a sweet tune as he cooks. (Note: the cooking should be actual so that the smells of the menudo fill the room.)*

Earl (*calling out to* **Esteban**)   The shoes! The shoes! Help me off with the damn shoes!

Esteban *reluctantly leaves his pot and goes to help* **Earl***. He starts trying to pull* **Earl***'s boots off as* **Earl** *moans.*

Esteban   Oh, Mr Earl, why you no come home when I tell you? Is no good to drink so much like that. You drink enough for ten men. We should have come home right after we make the phone call. Now we have miss everyone. Your father is gone. Your brother is gone.

Earl (*struggling to kick his boots off*)   They've always been gone! They were never here to begin with!

Esteban   I feel bad we no here when your father they take him away. We should have been here for that, Mr Earl. To see your father off.

Earl (*kicking out at* **Esteban**)   Get away from me! Just get the hell away! It's like being with a woman, being around you!

Esteban   You cry for help – you chase me away. You chase me away – you cry for help. It's the same as your father.

Earl (*sitting up with a struggle*)   I am nothing like the old man! Get that into your fry-brain little mind! We're as different as chalk and cheese! I am nothing like the old man!

Esteban *backs off and returns to his cooking. Pause as* **Earl** *finishes kicking off one boot. He sits up on edge of bed, tries to steady his dizziness, clutches his head in agony.*

Earl   Oh, my God! Feels like an ax in the back of my head. How'd you allow me to get into this kinda condition? Huh? You watch after Henry like a damn nanny goat, then you just turn my ass loose in every strange bar in creation. Where in the hell are your sense of values, man?

Esteban   You wanted to go to those bars, Mr Earl. You wanted to visit all of Henry's old bars. That's what you told me.

Earl   Now, why would I tell you something like that? Why would I give a shit about Henry's old bars?

Esteban   You are asking me this?

Earl   I'm asking you. Yeah.

Esteban   Menudo is almost ready.

Earl   I don't want any goddamn menudo! I'm asking you a question! Why would I wanna go around to Henry's old bars?

Esteban   I have no idea, Mr. Earl. Maybe you thought you would – discover something.

Earl   Discover? Discover what?

Esteban   Something about Henry.

Earl (*gives up pursuit*)   Ah, shit.

Esteban   Menudo will cure you.

Earl   I told you, I don't want any a that goddamn stuff! What is that junk anyway? Boiled cow bellies? Where do you people come up with this shit? Who first thought of that? Boiled cow intestines! Jesus. It's primitive.

Esteban   It will take away the pain.

Earl   I'm not eating any boiled cow guts! The brain of a man does not respond to the guts of a cow! Don't you know anything?

Pause. **Esteban** *keeps stirring the menudo.* **Earl** *nurses his head.*

Esteban   You are right about one thing.

Earl   What's that?

Esteban   You are nothing like your father. You are worse than your father. At least with Henry you could have a conversation.

Earl   Oh yeah, he was a real conversationalist, wasn't he? Real gift for gab, old Henry. Just talk your head off on any damn subject. (*Pause.*) What was in it for you, anyway?

Esteban   *Mande?*

Earl   What was in it for you? You and Henry. I mean all that sacrifice. Taking all that shit off a him all that time. What'd you ever have coming back?

Esteban (*keeps stirring pot*)   I no understand, Mr Earl.

Earl   What satisfaction could you possibly get outta serving a man who was so damn ungrateful!

Esteban   It is like – feeding livestock – you know?

Earl   Feeding livestock?

Esteban   Birds.

Earl   Birds?

Esteban   They do nothing. They – live, that is all. They are just there. But they need you. They look to you. They wait for you by the fence. They know you bring them something. Every day they are there at the same time – waiting. They know the hour you will appear. Mr Henry, he use to wait for me like that. I would see him standing by that window, looking toward my trailer. I would never tell him I see him waiting like that. He would be embarrassed; angry. But he look for me. I was the only one. He have no one else. Then – sometimes late at night, I come over and we sit. We just sit here at that table, facing the moon. We listen to the radio. We no speak. Sometimes we no speak for hours. Just listen. Music from deep in Mexico.

Earl   But every now and then you'd have a conversation, right? You were saying you used to have conversations –

Esteban   Sometimes. Sometimes Henry he ask me about my pueblo – where I come from. My people, my family. He never talk about himself. He say he have no past. Mostly we just listen. Dogs. Coyotes. *La musica.* It was peaceful.

Earl   Peaceful? Henry?

Esteban   The two of us.

Earl   Peaceful. That'd be something, wouldn't it?

Esteban   What?

Earl   Peace. (*Pause.*)

Esteban   Ay. Menudo.

Returns to stove. **Esteban** *keeps stirring pot.* **Earl** *gazes around room, then suddenly notices the missing toolbox and photo album. He stands fast and moves shakily toward table.*

Earl   That son of a bitch took everything! Look! He took the tools and the album. And the bottle! He took the damn bottle too! Those didn't belong to him! Nobody said he could have that stuff! Who in the hell does he think he is? He's absconded with everything! Look at this!

Esteban   Maybe he was only cleaning up.

Earl   Cleaning up? He's ripped me off! He doesn't deserve any of that stuff! That was mine! That belonged to me! I inherited it fair and square! I was the one who stuck it out here with Henry. Not him!

Esteban   I am very sorry we miss him. I wanted to say goodbye.

Earl   Who?

Esteban   Mr Henry.

Earl   He was dead! You don't say goodbye to a dead man! It's too late. I'm talking about my brother now. My living, breathing conniving brother!

Esteban   In my village we always say goodbye to the dead.

Earl   This is not your village. We're across the river here.

Esteban   They will come back to haunt you if you do not say goodbye.

Earl   Will you knock it off with that! Dead is dead, all right? Finished. *Terminado.*

Esteban   Maybe.

Earl   Maybe nothing.

Esteban   Maybe Henry was waiting to say goodbye and we weren't here.

Earl   Jesus H. Christ! Just – just – stir your damn pot, will you! Just –

He sits down heavily in upstage chair and holds his throbbing head between his hands. Long pause as **Esteban** *continues to stir his pot.*

Esteban (*stirring*)   We had a cousin, Manolito, once, who died from a green snake. No one said goodbye to him. There was superstition about the snake and no one said goodbye. The next day a hawk appeared above the door of his uncle's house. Every day the hawk would shit on his uncle's head just as he stepped outside. Every single day. That went on for over a month. This is the kind of thing that can happen when you don't say goodbye to the dead. You get shit on by a hawk.

Short pause. **Earl** *lowers his hands and looks at* **Esteban***. Suddenly* **Ray** *enters with a bag of groceries and closes door behind him. He stops and stares at* **Earl***.* **Earl** *stays seated.* **Esteban** *turns and stares at* **Ray***.*

Ray   How's it going?

He crosses to refrigerator, opens it and starts unloading groceries into it. Pause.

Earl   'How's it going?' That's all you've got to say? 'How's it going?'

Ray (*unloading groceries*)   Well, I was thinking about 'How ya doing?' or 'What's goin' on?' or 'Where you been so long?'

Earl   What're you doing back here?

Ray   Stockin' up the larder. Puttin' in a few supplies. I made kind of a big decision last night. It just came on me.

Earl   Yeah, what decision's that?

Ray   I'm gonna stay awhile.

Pause. **Earl** *stares at* **Ray**, *who keeps unloading groceries and putting them in fridge.* **Esteban** *keeps stirring.*

Earl   You're gonna stay?

Ray   Yep.

Earl   You mean here? You're gonna stay here in this house? Henry's house?

Ray   Yep. I like it here.

Earl   Oh, so now you like it here. It's warm and cozy.

Ray   I dunno. I feel – some kind of connection here.

Earl   Connection?

Ray   Yep.

Earl   I suppose you felt some kind of 'connection' to the tools and the photo album too, huh? And the bottle. My bottle.

Ray   Oh – yeah, well – I gave those away.

Earl (*moving toward* **Ray**)   What?

Ray   I gave 'em away to that taxicab driver.

Earl   What taxicab driver!

Ray   You know, the guy who uh – took Dad fishing. (*Pause.*)

Earl   What're you talking about?

Ray   The guy – the driver who came and picked Dad up. You know.

Pause.

Earl   You – found him?

Ray   Yep.

Earl   What do you mean? How'd you find him?

Ray   Tracked him down. Like I said. Through the company. Made some phone calls down there at the Sonic. I looked all over the place for you guys but I guess you were, uh 'celebrating' or something, huh?

Earl   You found the taxicab driver who took Henry fishing?

Ray   That's what I said, yeah. Amazing, huh?

Earl   You actually went all the way out of your way to find the taxicab driver who took Henry fishing?

Ray *finishes with groceries, closes refrigerator, takes a Coke with him, crosses to* **Earl**, *stops in front of him and raps on his forehead like he was knocking on a door.*

Ray   What is it, Earl – liquor or genetics that makes you so thick?

He crosses to table, sits and opens Coke, takes a drink.

Earl   So – so what'd he do? You talk to him?

Ray   Yeah. Sure I talked to him. What is that stink?

Esteban   Menudo.

Ray   Really stinks.

Earl (*moving toward* **Ray**)   So, what'd he say – this taxicab driver? He tell you anything different than what I told you?

Ray   Now why would he do that?

Earl   I don't know why he'd do that! Just to – confuse the issue probably. People are always making up stuff.

Ray   What issue?

Earl   You know – the issue – the whole situation. The perdicament here!

Ray   I didn't know there was a perdicament here, Earl.

Earl   There isn't a perdicament here but he could've made it seem like there was a perdicament here! He could've twisted things around!

Ray   He just told me what happened, that's all. Simple story.

Earl (*pause*)   So – Everything matched up, right? I mean everything he told you was the same thing I told you, right?

Ray   Pretty much. (*Pause.*)

Earl   What the hell are you doing giving away our father's belongings to a complete stranger? That's what I wanna know. What kind of a stunt is that?

Ray   I didn't think they meant anything to you.

Earl   There were photographs in there going back to the turn of the century!

Ray   Yeah. That's a long time ago.

Earl   You're goddamn right that's a long time ago! Those photographs are irreplaceable. Now some total stranger's got ahold of them. An outsider!

Ray   Well, he can always make up some kind of a story about them.

Earl   What's that supposed to mean?

Ray   He can tell people they're pictures of his family. His ancestors. He can make up a whole tall tale.

Earl   Why would he wanna do that?

Ray   Maybe he's got no family. Maybe he needs to make one up.

Earl   If he's got no family he can't make one up! That's not something you make up outta thin air! You can't make that stuff up. It's too complicated!

Ray   People will believe anything, Earl. You know that. Look at all the stuff you've told me.

Earl   What stuff?

Ray   Over the years. All the bullshit you've told me. I believed every word.

Earl   You know what? You're beginning to make me a little bit sick to my stomach. Ever since you arrived here. You come in here with this – this – 'atmosphere' around you. This suspicion. Right off the bat. Everybody's under suspicion. You don't have one clue about what's gone on here – about what me and Esteban have been through. You just waltz in here and start judging – passing judgment!

Ray   I've got a clue, Earl. I've got a big clue.

Pause. The brothers stare at each other. **Esteban** *very quietly stirs his pot, trying to become invisible. Pause.* **Earl** *shakes his head in disgust.*

Esteban   Menudo is almost ready!

Earl (*turning on* **Esteban**)   I don't want any menudo! I told you that! I'm not interested in menudo! If you mention menudo one more time I'm gonna rip your guts out and throw them in that pot!

He clutches his head in pain. He returns to **Henry**'s *bed and crashes.*

Earl (*writhing on bed*)   Oh, my God. Oh, my God, my God, my God!

Ray (*at table, sipping Coke*)   Too much party, Earl? You're a little old to be hitting the sauce like that. What were you, uh, 'celebrating' exactly? The removal of the corpse?

Earl (*on bed*)   You get outta here now! Go someplace else! There's lots of motels in this town. You just get outta here!

Ray   Or were you, uh – thinking maybe you got away with something?

Pause. **Earl** *struggles to sit up on the bed. He finally makes it and sits there, facing* **Ray**.

Earl   What'd this joker tell you? This taxicab driver? He told you something, didn't he?

Ray   Now, what would he tell me, Earl?

Earl (*standing, shaky*)   He put some idea in your head!

Ray   I got my own ideas, Earl. I don't need any new ones.

Earl   He was an idiot, that guy! A total idiot!

Ray   Oh, so you met him, then? You were here the same time he was, huh?

Earl   I didn't – I didn't meet him! Henry told me about him.

Ray   Henry?

Earl   I mean – Esteban! Esteban told me he was an idiot! (*To* **Esteban**.) Didn't you? (*No answer from* **Esteban**.) Didn't you tell me that? You told me the guy was a total jerk.

Ray   Well, which was it – a jerk or an idiot?

Earl (*to* **Ray**)   You're trying to turn this thing into something that it wasn't!

Ray   What was it, Earl? What exactly was it?

Earl *charges* **Ray** *but* **Ray** *dodges him quickly and is out of the chair in a flash.*

Earl   I want you outta here! I want you the hell outta here now!

He crashes into the table and crumples on top of it, exhausted. **Ray** *slowly circles him. Pause.* **Esteban** *turns the heat off under his pot.* **Ray** *keeps circling* **Earl**, *who remains sprawled out on top of the table.*

Esteban   I will come back later.

Ray (*keeps circling*)   No, you just keep cooking, Esteban. No reason to stop cooking.

Esteban   I think I should go back to my trailer, Mr Ray.

Earl (*collapsed on table*)   My legs. I can't feel my legs!

Ray   Get off the table, Earl. What do you think this is, a flophouse or something? A drunk-tank!

Earl   Something's happened to my legs!

Ray   Get off the table!

*Ray kicks Earl's feet out from under him. Earl crashes to the floor.
Esteban moves toward door. Pause.*

Esteban   I have no reason to be here, Mr Ray.

Ray   None of us do, Esteban. That's the truth of it, isn't it?
We're all just hanging around now. The old man's dead.

*Esteban crosses back to stove, turns it on and continues stirring pot.
Earl stays on floor.*

Earl (*on floor*)   Something's really gone wrong with my legs,
Ray. I'm not kidding you. I don't know what it is.

Ray   Get up off the floor, Earl. You're a full-grown man.

Earl (*stays on floor*)   I – I think we should call somebody.

Ray   Get up off the floor!

*He kicks Earl hard in the ribs. Earl struggles to the downstage chair
and drags himself up into it. Esteban keeps stirring.*

Ray   You know what I think? I think it's time we straightened
up in here, don't you? Get a little order. I mean if I'm gonna
be living here I'd like to have a little order. Scrub the floors
maybe. The windows. Brighten the place up a bit. What do
you think? How 'bout it, Esteban? You got a bucket around?
A mop?

Pause. Esteban and Earl stare at him like he's lost his mind.

Ray   No mop?

Esteban   No mop, Mr Ray.

Ray   No mop. How 'bout some rags, then? Must be some old
rags around. Well, this will work.

*He rips the apron off Esteban and balls it up. He crosses to Earl,
crushing the apron between his hands.*

Ray   Now, here's what we're gonna do, Earl. This is my house
now. So I want it clean. It's only natural. I want it spotless.
I want it so you can eat right off the floor. So you can see the

sun bounce off every little nook and cranny. Now, I want you to take this apron and get it wet.

Ray *grabs* **Earl** *by the hair, shoves the apron into* **Earl**'s *face and drags* **Earl** *over to the tub. He turns the hot water on and forces* **Earl** *to soak the apron in it.*

Esteban (*at stove, crossing himself frantically*)   Jesus, Maria, Jose! Jesus, Maria, Jose! Jesus, Maria, Jose!

Ray (*at tub, forcing* **Earl**)   Get it wet now, Earl. Get it nice and wet and wring it out. Scrub every inch of this floor till it shines like new money! That's what I want you to do, Earl. I want you to do that for me, right now.

Pause. **Earl** *follows* **Ray**'s *orders.* **Ray** *smiles at* **Esteban** *and crosses to him.* **Ray** *smells the pot of menudo and pats* **Esteban** *on the back.*

Ray   Stuff really stinks bad, Esteban. Is it supposed to smell like that? Smells like something dead.

Earl *begins slowly scrubbing floor with wet apron, on his hands and knees.* **Ray** *moves to tub and shuts the water off.*

Ray   This whole house stinks. Why is that? Is that from all your cooking, Esteban – over the years? Years and years of soups and chili and beans and shit? All that cooking. For what? What'd you think you were gonna do? Save Henry's puny life? Is that what you thought?

Earl   I'm really serious about my legs, Ray. They've gone numb.

Ray *suddenly kicks the bed.* **Earl** *stops scrubbing but stays on his hands and knees.* **Esteban** *is backed up to the stove.*

Ray   Just keep scrubbing, Earl. We may have to disinfect this whole house. We may have to tear the walls down and rebuild the whole son of a bitch. Just to get the stink outta here. What is that stink? Can't you smell that? What smells like that? Maybe it's you, Earl. Is it you that smells like that?

Earl *starts scrubbing the floor again.* **Ray** *goes to him, bends down and smells* **Earl** *all over as* **Earl** *continues scrubbing.*

Ray   Esteban – come over here and smell Earl. See what you think. Come on over here.

Esteban *reluctantly crosses to* **Earl** *and* **Ray**.

Ray (*to* **Esteban**) Now, just bend down here and smell him. I can't tell anymore. I've lost track. What's he smell like to you?

Esteban *bends over and smells* **Earl**, *who continues scrubbing floor.* **Esteban** *straightens up and stares at* **Ray**.

Ray   Well?

Esteban   Just – like a man, Mr Ray.

Ray   A man! Is that what a man smells like?

He bends over and takes a long whiff of **Earl**, *who keeps right on scrubbing through all this.* **Ray** *straightens up.*

Ray   Nah, I dunno – smells rotten to me.

Earl *stops scrubbing.*

Earl   Look – I'm not feeling so good. That tequila messed me up. I'm not used to that stuff.

Ray *kicks* **Earl** *in the ass.*

Ray   Keep scrubbing, Earl! Just keep yer nose to the grindstone. There's a lotta territory to cover here. Lots of square footage.

Earl *starts scrubbing floor again.* **Esteban** *returns to his place by the stove.* **Ray** *moves around the room.*

Ray   You remember how Mom used to work at it, don't ya?

Earl (*scrubbing*)   Mom?

Ray   Yeah. You remember how she used to scrub, day in and day out. Scrub, scrub, scrub.

Earl   I don't remember.

Ray   You remember. You remember how she used to get everything spit-shined and polished – everything gleaming.

The floors. The curtains. The tablecloth starched. All the glasses shining.

Throughout this sequence the tempo of **Earl**'s *scrubbing increases with the force of* **Ray**'s *pursuit.* **Ray** *moves freely around the space.*

Earl   No –

Ray   You remember. Potatoes steaming on the plates. Carrots. Everything waiting. Everything perfect and just waiting like some kind of picture. You remember all that.

Earl   No –

Ray   And then – I used to think – I used to think she was doing all that for us, you know. You and me. I used to think she was going through all this work – all this preparation for us. And then, one day, it just – hit me. I don't know why. I just suddenly saw that it wasn't for us at all. It was for him. It was for Henry. Everything. All those hours and hours, slaving away – slaving away. It was for him.

Earl   I don't remember that.

Ray   And then – and then, here he'd come! Bustin' in the door. You remember.

He rushes to the door, opens and slams it, then turns himself into drunken **Henry***, staggering into the room.* **Earl** *keeps scrubbing.*

Ray   (*impersonating* **Henry**)   'What the hell is everyone waitin' on me for? What're you waitin' on? The food's hot! Sit down and eat the food. Jesus H. Christ! You'd think this was some kinda goddamn formal dinner here or something. You're hungry, aren't ya? Sit down and eat!' (*Drops impersonation.*) And then everybody'd scramble to the table while he'd stomp the shit off his boots and throw his coat on the floor. You remember that? You remember how we'd all just sit there staring down into our napkins while he went on ranting and raving about the lack of rain or the price of citrus or the cost of feeding useless sons! Do you remember that, Earl? Do you remember that at all?

Earl (*still scrubbing*)   No, I don't remember! I don't remember any of that. You must've been alone. I must've been out someplace.

Ray   You were there, Earl. You were there the whole time. I remember your breath. The sound of your breath. Chopping away. I remember thinking, 'He must be just as scared as me to be breathing like that. Just as full of terror!' But then I thought, 'No, that's not possible. He's bigger than me. He's my big brother. How could he be scared?' And when she started screaming I thought, 'Earl's gonna stand up for her. Earl's gonna take the weight. Earl's gonna stop him somehow!'

Earl   I wasn't there for that! I was never there!

Ray   Because I knew, see – I knew I didn't have a chance against him. I barely came up to his waist. All I could do is watch! And there she was – on the floor! Just like you, Earl. Just like you are now. Backed up under the sink! Crushed. He was kicking her, Earl! He was kicking her just like this!

He starts savagely kicking **Earl** *all over the stage.* **Earl** *scrambles on his hands and knees but* **Ray** *is relentless.* **Esteban** *cowers and stays clear.*

Ray   And every time he kicked her his rage grew a little bit and his face changed! His eyes bulged out and the blood rushed into his neck! And her blood was flying all over the kitchen, Earl!

Earl (*scrambling away on hands and knees*)   That wasn't me that was doing that! That wasn't me! That was him!

Ray *suddenly stops kicking* **Earl**. *They are both panting for breath.*

Ray   And still I kept thinking – I kept thinking, 'Sooner or later Earl's gonna step in. Earl's gonna stop him. Earl's not going to let this happen.' And just then – I looked out the kitchen window and I saw your car – your little white Chevy. Kicking up dust the whole length of the hayfield. And that's the last time I saw you, Earl. That's the last time I saw you for a long, long while.

Earl (*still on floor*)   I never ran! I never ran!

Short pause, then **Henry** *suddenly blasts through the door with* **Conchalla** *close behind, still wrapped up in the blanket.* **Ray** *moves immediately extreme downstage and becomes witness again. He faces the audience the whole time.* **Earl** *remains on the floor. Lights shift. Soft spot on* **Ray.** **Esteban** *hangs near the stove.* **Conchalla** *goes to the bed and flops down on it.* **Henry** *approaches* **Earl.** *Both* **Henry** *and* **Conchalla** *are as drunk as the last time we saw them.* **Henry** *stops in front of* **Earl** *and sniffs the air.*

Henry   What stinks? What's that stink in here?

Esteban   Menudo, Mr Henry.

Henry   Well, turn that shit off! Smells like a goddamn Tijuana whorehouse in here. Turn it off!

Esteban *turns off the stove.*

Esteban   I was making it for Mr Earl.

Henry   What's a matter with 'Mr Earl'? What's he doing crawling around on my floor? (*To* **Earl**.) What're you doing down there?

Earl   I've lost track.

Henry   Well, get the hell up off my floor! This isn't some kind of a New York City crash pad or something. Have some respect. I've got a woman in the house, in case you didn't notice.

Conchalla (*calling out from bed*)   A woman! A woman in the house!

Earl *drags himself up from floor and just stands there.*

Henry (*to* **Earl**)   What's the deal here anyway? You showing up outta the blue like this. What's the big idea?

Earl   Esteban told me it was an emergency.

Henry   Emergency! He's a Mexican! Everything's an emergency with them.

Earl   He said you'd disappeared.

Henry   Since when did you ever give two shits whether I disappeared or not? I haven't seen hide nor hair of you – for how long's it been now?

Earl   I forget.

Henry   Yeah. Me too.

Earl   I wasn't – sure you wanted to see me.

Henry   Oh, is that right? You weren't sure. Well, let's get clear about this then. Let's get this straight once and for all. Far as I'm concerned you never even existed! You were one big bad mistake! All right? Does that make any kind of sense to you at all?

Earl   Yeah. Yeah, that makes sense. That explains a whole lot.

Henry   Good. Now you can clear on outta here because everything's just hunky-dory. Why in the hell does that stuff stink so bad?

He crosses to **Esteban**. **Conchalla** *giggles and turns over on the bed.*

Henry (*to* **Esteban**)   What're you doin' here anyway? Why are you always here, stickin' yer nose into my business? Don't you have your own place? What is it about my place that's so damn attractive?

Conchalla   There is a woman! A woman in the house!

Henry (*to* **Conchalla**)   You pipe down!

Conchalla *rises from the bed and offers her arm out to* **Esteban**.

Conchalla   I will take you to your trailer, Esteban. Come on.

Esteban *starts to cross to door but* **Conchalla** *intercepts him and throws her arms around him. Holding* **Esteban**.

Conchalla   I will take you there and bounce you on my knees!

She squeezes **Esteban** *in a bear hug and bounces him up and down.*

Conchalla (*as she bounces* **Esteban**)   Wouldn't you like some bouncing? I will bounce you all night long until the sun explodes! Wouldn't you like that? Wouldn't you like some of that, Esteban?

Henry   Knock it off! Knock it off!

Conchalla *stops bouncing* **Esteban** *and throws him backward onto the bed.*

Henry   He doesn't need any bouncing!

Conchalla *slowly approaches* **Esteban** *on bed.*

Conchalla   He looks to me like a man who could use some bouncing. Look how flat he is.

Henry   If there's any bouncing going on here I'll be the one in charge of it.

Conchalla (*turning to* **Henry**)   Oh, you'll be the one?

Henry   That's right.

Now **Conchalla** *approaches* **Henry**, *slow and seductive.* **Esteban** *gets up from bed and heads for the door.*

Conchalla (*approaching* **Henry**)   You'll be the one in charge of bouncing? The Captain of Bouncing! I didn't know dead men were any good at bouncing. I thought their bouncing days were over.

She exits with **Esteban**.

Henry (*appealing to* **Earl**)   There she goes again! She won't give it up. She goes around and around and around about it. She ate my fish, you know.

Earl   What?

Henry   My fish I caught. She ate it. Raw! She's a barbarian!

He crosses to bed and collapses on it. Pause as **Earl** *just stands there, not knowing what to do with his father.*

Earl   You need anything, Dad?

Henry (*stays on bed*)   What!

Earl   You need something? You want me to get you something?

Henry   Yeah – most likely I do. Most likely I need something. I've got that feeling. What would it be? What would it be that I need?

Pause. **Earl** *moves closer to* **Henry**, *who remains crumpled on the bed.* **Earl** *stops.*

Earl   You need a blanket or something?

Henry   She's got the blanket! She takes everything. The blanket. The bottle. My fish.

Earl   Who is she, anyway?

Henry   Who is she?

Earl   Yeah. I mean – I had no idea you were living with a woman.

Henry   I'm not living with her! Don't be ridiculous. How could you live with something like that?

Earl   Well, whatever you call it.

Henry   You don't call it living!

He rolls over and sits up unsteadily. He stares at **Earl**.

Henry   I don't suppose you've got a bottle, do ya?

Earl   No, I –

Henry   Nah, you wouldn't have a bottle. You don't have a pot to piss in.

He gets up and staggers toward refrigerator. He opens it and stares into it. **Earl** *watches him. Staring into fridge.*

Henry   What're you doin' out here, anyway? Why'd you come all the way out here?

Earl   Esteban – He called me. He said you were in trouble or something. He said you'd disappeared.

Henry *laughs and slams refrigerator shut. Turns to* **Earl**.

Henry   Disappeared! Disappeared?

Earl   Yeah. That's what he said.

Henry (*staggers toward* **Earl**)   Have you ever known anybody who's disappeared? Huh? (*He stops.*) Just – vanished?

Earl   No –

Henry   No. That's not possible, is it? Is that a possible thing for a human being? Just – disappear?

Earl   I don't know. I mean, I guess there have been –

Henry   What?

Earl   Cases.

Henry   Disappearing cases?

Earl   Yeah.

Henry *staggers closer to* **Earl** *and stops.*

Henry   Are you – are you seeing me, right now?

Earl   What?

Henry   Are you seeing me – perceiving me as we speak?

Earl   Well, yeah – Sure.

Henry   You're sure?

Earl   Yeah. Why?

Henry   You're convinced that I'm standing here before you? That I'm an actuality in this world?

Earl   Yeah.

Henry   What's giving you that impression?

Earl   What?

Henry   That I'm here. That I'm real? What's convincing you of that?

Earl   I – I recognize you.

Henry   You do?

Earl   Yeah.

Henry   What do you recognize? What is it?

Earl   I remember –

Henry   What?

Earl   Your voice. Your eyes. The – smell.

Henry   The smell? What smell?

Earl   That – that –

Henry   Booze?

Earl   No.

Henry   What, then?

Earl   Some – some – scent of you.

Henry   A scent? You mean like a dog or something?

Earl   No –

Suddenly **Henry** *throws his arms around* **Earl** *and squeezes him in a bear hug.* **Earl** *panics but can't get out of it.*

Henry (*squeezing* **Earl**)   You mean like a dog, don't ya? Like a mad dog?

Earl (*struggling*)   No! Let go a me for God's sake!

Henry (*still squeezing* **Earl** *in his grip*)   Like a dead man! Is that what you think? You ever known a dead man with a grip like this?

Earl *finally breaks free and shoves* **Henry** *back. They stand apart.*

Henry   You shouldn't take it personal.

Earl   That woman –

Henry   Yeah. She's somethin', huh? Conchalla Lupina. Ever seen anything like her?

Earl   No – no, I never did.

Henry   She'd scare the pants off a natural man. You probably couldn't handle a woman like that.

Earl   No, probably not. Where'd you meet her, anyway?

Henry   Where'd I meet her? Where do ya suppose I'd meet her?

Earl   I have no idea.

Henry *begins slowly to approach* **Earl***. At the same time, the door swings open and* **Conchalla** *is standing there watching.* **Henry***'s back is to her, but* **Earl** *can see her in the doorway. She takes sips from a bottle of tequila.*

Henry (*as he moves to* **Earl**)   I was − 'obliterated', as they say. Absolutely sloshed. Been in and outta that drunk-tank down there for over a month. This time though − I woke up − she was on top a me. (*Laughs.*) She had me straddled!

Earl (*trying to end the story*)   All right, all right!

Conchalla (*giggles in doorway*)   He couldn't resist me! I was too much woman!

Henry *doesn't look back to* **Conchalla** *but keeps his focus on* **Earl***.* **Earl** *backs away.*

Henry   I couldn't resist. It's true. There she was − big as day!

Earl   I − I don't really wanna hear about it, okay?

Conchalla *enters room and closes door behind her. She keeps sipping from bottle and smiling at* **Earl***.*

Henry   Big as the damn Sangre de Cristo mountains! Right on top a me. What could I do?

Conchalla   He was whimpering when they threw him in. Hunched up in a corner, whining like a puppy.

Henry   I wasn't whimpering. I had the shakes. Cold.

Conchalla   He was whimpering.

Henry (*approaching* **Earl**)   Huddled up − trying to get some warmth. Just trying to find some warmth − that's all.

Conchalla   I gave him warmth.

Earl (*trying to escape them*)   That's enough!

Conchalla   I gave him so much warmth, he passed out. He couldn't take my warmth!

*She giggles as she and **Henry** close in on **Earl**.*

Henry   I could take it. I could take it.

Conchalla   When I dismounted him, his heart stopped. His breath. Nothing was moving.

Earl   I don't wanna hear anymore of this! I don't wanna hear anymore! All right? Stop telling me about this! Just stop telling me about all this!

Henry *and* **Conchalla** *stop suddenly.* **Henry** *notices* **Conchalla**'s *bottle and approaches her, trying to get a hit off it, but she hides it behind her back.*

Earl (*after pause*)   Look – for some strange reason or other, I still remember my mother, okay?

Henry   Your mother?

Earl   Yeah. Yeah, that's right. My mother. I can still – picture her. I can – see her. I can –

Henry   Your mother.

Earl   She was always –

Henry   What?

Earl   Faithful. She was always faithful. No matter what. I remember her now. I remember her on her hands and knees.

Henry   Your mother. That little shit.

Conchalla *giggles, drinks, goes to bed and flops down on it.*

Henry   Another traitor. Locked me out of my own house! That's what she did. Locked me out!

Earl   I remember that too.

Henry   You remember nothin'! Your 'mother'. Wasn't for her, I wouldn't be in this mess I'm in right now. This whole situation!

Earl   How is she to blame for that?

Henry   She caused me to leave! She caused me to pack on outta there! What'd ya think? You think I wanted to wander around this Christless country for twenty-some years like a refugee? Like some miserable fuckin' exile? Huh? You think I wanted that? She did that to me! She banished me! She turned me out!

Earl   You broke the place up. You smashed all the windows!

Henry   SHE LOCKED ME OUT!

He collapses, grabs onto the upstage chair and crashes to his knees. **Earl** *moves toward him, but* **Conchalla** *stops him.*

Conchalla   Don't touch him!

Henry (*on his knees, clutching chair*)   She locked me out, that's what she did to me. Locked me out completely.

Conchalla   Now he will start to crumble – to whimper. The same. Always the same.

Earl   Dad? You want a doctor or something? You wanna go to the hospital?

Conchalla *laughs and drinks from bottle.*

Conchalla   The hospital! He is way beyond the hospital!

She grabs **Henry** *by the chest with tremendous force and lifts him up to the table. She lays him out on his back on the table as* **Earl** *watches helplessly.*

Earl   What the hell're you doing to him! Haven't you done enough damage already?

Conchalla *giggles and strokes* **Henry**'s *hair gently. Then she lifts his head and starts pouring the tequila into his mouth very gently, like medicine.* **Henry** *gurgles.*

Conchalla   Damage? I have done no damage. I am just
watching out for the dead. Do you know how much trouble
that is? Watching – always watching? It takes a lot of time.
A lot of patience.

Earl   Stop it! Stop giving him that!

He lunges toward **Conchalla***, trying to grab the bottle away from her,
but she lets out a bloodcurdling scream and freezes* **Earl** *in his tracks. She
giggles. She strokes* **Henry***'s face very gently.*

Conchalla   I will show you your father. You see him now?
You see how he looks to me. Helpless. Hoping. Dreaming.
Wishing for death. Wishing for some way out. (*Stroking* **Henry***'s
head.*) It takes courage, no? I gave him courage. A drowned
man. He comes up for air. He gasps –

She keeps pouring tequila down **Henry** *as she straddles him. Stroking*
Henry*'s head.*

Conchalla   Now he begins to go back home. Now – he
begins to return. You will see. He remembers now.

Henry (*spitting to get his throat clear*)   I remember – the day
I died – she was on the floor.

Conchalla (*gently*)   Now, he sees.

Henry *sits up on table with* **Conchalla** *supporting him and gently
stroking his head as* **Earl** *watches.*

Henry   I remember the floor – was yellow – I can see the
floor and – her blood – her blood was smeared across it. I
thought I'd killed her – but it was me. It was me I killed.

Conchalla *kisses* **Henry** *lightly on the forehead and lifts him off the
table.* **Henry** *stands there, looking out.*

Henry   I can see her eyes – peering up at me. Her swollen
eyes. She just – stays there, under the sink. Silent. Balled up
like an animal. Nothing moving but her eyes. She sees me. She
knows. I can tell she knows. She sees me dying! Right there in
front of her. She watches me pass away! There's nothing she

can do. And then − there's this flash of grief − from her. Grief! Why would she grieve for me?

Earl *heads for the door.*

Earl   I can't listen to this anymore!

Conchalla *moves fast in front of* **Earl** *and stops him.*

Conchalla (*to* **Earl**)   You watch.

Henry   I ran out into the yard and I remember − I remember this − death. I remember it now − cut off. Everything − far away. Birds. Trees. Sky. Removed! Everything − out beyond reach. And I ran. I ran to the car and I drove. I drove for days with the windows wide open. The wind beating across my eyes − my face. I had no map. No destination. I just drove.

Conchalla *begins humming a death song and sways from side to side. She moves to* **Henry** *and hands him the bottle.* **Henry** *takes it and drinks.*

Henry (*to* **Earl**)   You could've stopped me then but you didn't.

Earl   What? What're you talking about?

Henry *turns with bottle and moves toward* **Earl** *but trying more to get to the bed.* **Earl** *backs away from him.* **Conchalla** *continues to sway and hum her song.*

Henry (*to* **Earl**)   You were there. You were there watching the whole time. I remember your beady eyes peering out at me from the hallway. You saw the whole thing.

Earl   I don't know what you're talking about!

Henry   You saw! I looked straight at you! You looked straight back. Your mother was screaming the whole time!

Earl   No! I was never there. I was never there for that!

Henry   You coulda stopped me but you didn't.

He almost loses his balance and crashes, but he staggers to the bed and goes down on top of it.

Earl   I couldn't. I – I – I was scared. I was – just – too – scared.

Henry   You were scared! A what? A me? You were scared of a dead man?

He takes a last giant pull on the bottle, then lies back and dies quietly. **Conchalla** *stops humming her song. She moves to* **Henry** *and covers him with the blanket. She turns to* **Earl***.*

Conchalla (*to* **Earl**)   The body – it stays. For three whole days no one must touch him. Not you. No one. You are the keeper. You watch now.

She exits. Pause. **Earl** *moves to the bed and sits down next to* **Henry***'s corpse, facing directly out to the audience. Pause.* **Ray** *turns to* **Earl** *but stays in his spot of light.* **Earl** *stares straight out.*

Ray   Well, you know me, Earl – I was never one to live in the past. That was never my deal. You know – you remember how I was.

Earl   Yeah. Yeah, right. I remember.

Lights fade slowly to black.